A PHOTOGRAPHIC GUIDE TO

WILDFLOWERS
OF
NEW ZEALAND

GEOFF & LIZ BRUNSDEN

D1382415

NH
NEW
HOLLAND

First published in 2004 by New Holland Publishers (NZ) Ltd
Auckland • Sydney • London • Cape Town

218 Lake Road, Northcote, Auckland, New Zealand
14 Aquatic Drive, Frenchs Forest, NSW 2086, Australia
86–88 Edgware Road, London W2 2EA, United Kingdom
80 McKenzie Street, Cape Town 8001, South Africa

www.newhollandpublishers.co.nz

Copyright © 2004 in text: Geoff and Liz Brunsden
Copyright © 2004 in photography: Geoff and Liz Brunsden
Additional photographs by Peter Johnson, as credited
Copyright © 2004 New Holland Publishers (NZ) Ltd

Managing editor: Matt Turner
Design and typesetting: Julie McDermid
Editor: Brian O'Flaherty

ISBN: 978 1869660 475

A catalogue record for this book is available from the National Library of
New Zealand.

Colour reproduction by PICA Colour Separation, Singapore
Printed by Times Offset (M) Sdn Bhd, Malaysia

10 9 8 7 6 5 4 3

Front cover photograph: *Malcomia maritima*
Back cover photograph: *Myosotidium hortensia*
Spine photograph: *Chrysanthemum leucanthemum*
Title page photograph: *Osteospermum fruticosum*

Contents

Preface 4

Introduction 4

What is a wildflower? 5

Selection of species 5

Gardening in New Zealand 5

Biosecurity..6

Wildflower habitats 6

How to use this book 7

The structure of wildflowers 7

Acknowledgements 11

Species photographs and descriptions

Blue/purple flowers 12–35

Red/pink flowers......................................36–60

Yellow/orange flowers...............................61–95

White flowers...96–123

Flowers with mixed colours..................124–135

Glossary..136

Further reading 138

Index 139

Preface

Lady Bird Johnson, wife of the late President Lyndon Johnson, helped create a passion for preserving wildflowers in the United States and wrote: 'Almost every person, from childhood on, has touched the untamed beauty of wildflowers: buttercup gold under a childish chin; the single drop of exquisite sweetness in the blossom of wild honeysuckle; the love-me, love-me-not philosophy of daisy petals.'

This is perhaps the main reason wildflowers capture our attention to such depth. As we move through the complexities of modern day life we tend to search back more and more into the peaceful memories of the past: uncluttered times of innocent youth, times when the pure fabric of being a child was just simply playing and dreaming in Grandma's garden or in a wide field on a beautiful summer's day.

We hope this book will capture this passion for you too.

Introduction

Geologically speaking, New Zealand is a relatively new landmass, separating from the Gondwana supercontinent some 80 million years ago and carried, by the process of seafloor spreading, into the South Pacific. Some of the original inhabitants survived this slow journey while other species did not.

Around 80 per cent of New Zealand's trees, ferns and flowering plants are endemic. The country's unique land-based flora and fauna evolved in the absence of mammalian plant browsers or predators, which made them very vulnerable to introduced predators and competitors, as well as to loss or alteration of habitat.

Before the arrival of Maori from eastern Polynesia in the 14th century AD around 78 per cent of the main islands was covered with forest. Maori introduced fire, food crops, a dog and a rat, which all helped alter the environment irrevocably. Before European settlement began in earnest in the early 19th century, around one-third of the forest had already been cleared. The settlers wasted no time in beginning their assault on the land, felling trees for timber, slashing and burning to create pasture, or mining and sluicing for coal and gold. Some 160 years later, around 23 per cent of the land remains forested.

It is possible that there existed meadow or prairie-type native wildflowers that disappeared as a result of this land clearance.

With the European settlers the introduction of flowers of the outside world to New Zealand began, most often for cultivation in farms and gardens. They have now become permanent residents, many with pleasurable links to our forebears' pioneering achievements, such as the marigolds of England or the poppies of Europe. However, with the pleasures came the pests. In came species that found a 'heaven from home' and that today grow in relentless abandon in environments wet and dry, field and forest, from North Cape to Bluff.

What is a wildflower?

For the purpose of this guide, true wildflowers are defined as flowering annuals and perennials that have not been modified by human intervention. However, to say that all of these species included here are genetically identical to their parents of centuries ago would be an open invitation to attract lively debate. Not only is there every probability that humans have at times assisted flowers with an occasional cross-pollination but specific selections have often been made to isolate a particular colour or form of plant. Also on occasions two species of wildflowers can cross-fertilise themselves to produce a desirable hybrid. Sometimes a species of wildflower can vary considerably from one part of the country to another, mostly in physical growth characteristics.

With the above in mind, in this guide we describe the common form of a particular species of wildflower as we find it in New Zealand today. These species are well deserved of the definition wildflower in that they come with characteristics such as being easy to grow, being tough survivors in sometimes harsh environments or have easily escaped the garden to readily colonise the environment.

Selection of species

The selection of species for this guide was no easy task. We set ourselves guidelines to include species that could be relatively easy to find on a trail from north to south. Here are flowers that can be found growing on the sides of roads and driveways, waste ground, coastal areas, parks, reserves, farm pastures and home gardens. They are plants that readily naturalise and colonise these areas, some being New Zealand natives but most exotic.

This is not a book describing common weeds found in New Zealand; however, where plants that are regarded as weeds have been included it is because they have some landscape value in terms of beauty, such as a field of buttercups. Also, we have avoided including bulbs, aquatic species, climbers and shrubs such as clematis or broom, although the odd one or two have crept in where they also have a landscape value and are very commonly found. Furthermore, alpine species are not included, as they are not commonly found without undertaking mountaineering expeditions! In short, here are the flowers you will find not far from the car, not far from the road and not far from home, but of course, due to limitations of space, not all you may be likely to find have been included.

Gardening in New Zealand

Gardening is a top leisure pursuit in New Zealand. The combination of a diverse range of climatic conditions and geographic regions with a long history of importing plant collections from all over the world has resulted in a fascinating range of landscape expressions. Over the last decade the cultivated use of wildflowers in the landscape has captured public awareness and appreciation. Many roading authorities, local councils and commercial enterprises are using wildflower collections not just for landscape enhancement but to save money by not mowing grass verges. Proudly, we can lay claim to introducing this concept into the commercial arena in New Zealand.

Biosecurity

The preservation of this country's existing flora as well as protection of our primary industries is critical. To our visitors coming in and our residents returning from overseas, please be aware of the consequences of bringing in unwanted seed species or disease. The biosecurity protection measures at the border are for the well and good of New Zealand and very strict import regulations are there to ensure that our environment is protected and preserved.

Wildflower habitats

The term habitat in this guide covers areas such as roadsides, waste ground, driveways, coastal areas, pasturelands, parks, reserves, commercial sites, meadow gardens and home gardens.

- *Roadsides:* refers to motorways, highways and country roads where along the shoulder or on the adjacent banks wildflowers can be found. It includes the road frontages of private property.
- *Waste ground:* refers to old dump sites, quarries and disused land and in many cases property surrounding industrial areas. Small pockets of this type of habitat throughout the country are perhaps the most common habitat for wildflowers.
- *Driveways:* refers mostly to long driveways into private property. These are common habitats for many wildflowers.
- *Coastal areas:* refers to rocky foreshores and sand dunes.
- *Pasturelands:* refers to grassed farm paddocks.
- *Parks and reserves:* refers to local council cultivated gardens and street-scaping of cities and towns as well as the large tracts of public land known as national parks, farm parks or forest parks.
- *Commercial sites:* refers to landscaping around areas that are commercially owned such as areas around shopping centres and commercial premises.
- *Meadow gardens:* refers to purposely planted wildflower meadows. These can be private or commercial.
- *Home gardens:* refers to privately owned gardens as well as those open to the general public.

Other good resource areas for finding wildflowers are old cemeteries, churchyards and both currently used and abandoned railway sidings. Wildflowers love sunshine, so seek them in these locations and you will be sure to find them.

Wildflowers by the sea.

How to use this book

For quick reference plants have first been categorised into five colour bands: blue/purple, red/pink, yellow/orange, white and finally mixed colours. Listing is then by botanical name alphabetically. To identify a flower, refer first to the colour section to compare the flower with the photographs. Complete the identification then by confirming the general habit of the plant, leaf description, flower description, time of flowering and any other characteristics.

While common names are highlighted, plants are listed by their botanical name so that affinities with related species can easily be seen. It is preferable to use the botanical name as the common name can vary considerably. Other common names or synonymous names are sometimes mentioned together with other members of the same species that are also commonly found. Common names, botanical names and references to other species are all listed in the index.

Technical terms have been kept to a minimum. It is not intended to give a complete botanical description of a plant but rather information to help you confirm that the plant you are trying to identify is the same as that shown in the photographs. A glossary of terms used is provided at the end of the book. Please note that metre has been abbreviated to m, centimetre to cm and millimetre to mm.

The structure of wildflowers

The wildflowers described come in an infinite variety of shapes, sizes and colours. A characteristic feature of them is that they produce flowers, meaning they belong in a group known as angiosperms, which is one of two groups of seed-producing plants. Gymnosperms form the second group and they have cones instead of flowers.

Wildflowers in a meadow.

Wildflowers all have five main parts or organs: roots, stems, leaves, flowers and fruit. In some cases one or more of these parts may not be apparent; for example, leaves or stems may be insignificant or in rare cases completely lacking.

Variations are closely linked to the way the plant lives. Many wildflowers use a source of stored food to put on a sudden burst of growth to flower very early in spring. Other wildflowers overwinter as dormant seeds to begin their growing cycle afresh once the conditions are favourable.

When looking to distinguish one wildflower from another it is probably the flower that is the most important organ to study first, followed by the stem and leaf.

Roots
The least commonly seen part of the wildflower is the roots. Roots perform two basic functions: anchorage for support and extraction of water and nutrients from the soil.

There are two main types of root systems in wildflowers and the types give a good indication of which group of flowering plant it belongs to. One group, the monocotyledons, has a fibrous root system. Here many equal-sized roots grow from the base of the stem that is often a swollen bulb. The other group, dicotyledons, has a taproot with a large central part from which smaller secondary roots grow.

Often roots have an extra function of storing a starchy food reserve to help survival through adverse weather conditions.

Wildflowers that grow on walls or rocky faces often have extra roots known as adventitious roots along their stems to provide better anchorage and support.

While the roots of the plant are important they have not usually been considered in the format of this guide.

Stems

There are three main functions of the stem: to provide support for leaves and flowers, to provide a transport system for the distribution of substances throughout the plant and to place the leaves in the best position to absorb sunlight.

For upright support the stem must be flexible and strong. The taller and more upright the plant, the stronger the stem. Fleshy stems often give way to hollow types as plant height increases. Some stems have extra reinforcing on their outsides, for example the square stems of the *Salvia* species. Not all plants have upright stems. The ground-creeping stems of plants such as periwinkle, *Vinca minor*, provide anchor roots at nodes along the stems, thereby colonising an area extensively.

Some plants are almost stemless in order to grow among other short plants or to be protected from wind exposure. The leaves of these plants are usually firm to the ground in a rosette pattern.

Leaves

Leaves are the main food-making organ of green plants. Shapes range from large, simple types to complex, finely divided, filamentous structures, with countless different shapes in between. It is both the shape of the leaves and the form of their edges that can significantly contribute to the accurate identification of wildflowers. Leaf types may be simple, with a single leaf blade and a stalk, or compound, with a number of leaflets arranged on a stalk. They can be arranged alternately or opposite

each other on a stem. Leaf types are further identified by their colour, texture and how they are attached to the stem; for example, a leaf can be sessile, meaning it is stalkless and arises straight from the stem.

Flowers

Flowers can grow singly or in groups. In most cases an individual flower has four main components arranged in whorls or spirals around a central stalk.

- The outermost part of the flower is the calyx. This is the protective part and consists of sepals that are usually green and are often fused together, giving a tube or cup-like form.
- Inside the calyx are the petals, usually larger and more brightly coloured to attract insects for pollination.
- Reproductive parts form the centre of the flower. The male parts, stamens, consist of slender stalks called filaments that end in a sac-like structure called an anther. Pollen grains are produced inside the anthers.
- In the centre of the flower also is the female reproductive organ consisting of the stigma, style and ovary, collectively called the pistil. Pollen grains attach themselves to the stigma and after fertilisation seeds develop.

Digitalis.

Wildflowers on a motorway median strip.

The arrangement and grouping of flowers is another useful way to identify wildflowers. The simplest arrangement is where plants have a solitary flower at the end of a stalk. More complex arrangements have flowers that grow directly along an upright stalk, called spikes. Flowers can also be arranged in terminal clusters on top of a flower stalk or on side shoots off the flower stalk.

Where flowers are borne on side shoots this is known as a raceme. Flower stalks that are multi-branched are panicles. Where the main stalk ends with a flower cluster with side branches this is called a cyme. An umbel is where a panicle consists of branches that all originate from the same point and end with the flowers all at the same level. Lastly, flowers such as the daisy family have a head or capitulum. This is where many small flowers are grouped together on a flattened receptacle and are surrounded by small, green bracts.

Fruit
Seeds of plants develop inside fruit that are made up of the original flower ovary wall. The seeds may be released individually once the fruit matures and bursts open, or may be dispersed intact as a whole fruit. There are many different kinds of fruit, dry and fleshy. Dry fruit types include nuts, pods and capsules. Fleshy fruit include berries and drupes. Mention of the fruit in this guide is only made if it is an important characteristic of the plant or to assist with identification.

Acknowledgements

We would like to thank the staff at the Auckland Regional Botanic Gardens and Mark Dean from Naturally Native New Zealand for their helpful advice. Also, Yvonne Carter and Bruce Waugh for their devoted assistance in locating wildflowers with us throughout New Zealand.

BLUE/PURPLE

Family Alliaceae. Agapanthus is a half-hardy, evergreen, perennial plant native to the Cape Province region of South Africa and is sometimes referred to as African lily. It grows in compact clumps up to 90 cm high from a tuberous rootstock of fleshy roots. The linear-lanceolate **leaves** are long, narrow and strap-shaped and up to 50 cm long. Showy, bright blue, sometimes white, clusters containing 12–30 funnel-shaped **flowers**, 3–5 cm long, are in rounded umbels and held well above the foliage. The long-stemmed **seed heads** can be dried for winter decoration. This very robust plant is often used for roadside and commercial landscaping as it is highly decorative, tough, and will flower all summer and autumn. Plants can be found in warmer areas throughout the country and home gardeners find them effective for erosion control. There are many cultivated forms, both dwarf and tall, coming in a range of blue and white shades. In New Zealand they are familiarly called aggies pants.

12

Cornflower *Centaurea cyanus*

Family Asteraceae. The cornflower is from a genus of over 600 species and is an annual, native to Great Britain and possibly parts of Europe. This is an erect, branched plant growing 60–90 cm high. Grey, cottony **leaves** are narrowly lanceolate and untoothed. The solitary **flower** head has rings of bright blue, tubular, deeply lobed, ray florets, 2–3 cm across. The outer florets are much longer than the inner. Flower bracts are narrowly fringed with brown or silver. Within this species plants with mixed flower colours from white through to purple and pink are also commonly found. Cornflowers are grown throughout the country in private gardens, parks, reserves and meadow gardens. Flowering is in spring and summer. In Great Britain the cornflower was once a troublesome weed of arable land but agricultural changes have been largely responsible for its decline. Plants with mixed colours are often called bachelor's buttons. The cornflower is a good cut flower and the blue species dries especially well.

Family Asteraceae. A branching, hardy, perennial plant with a fleshy taproot, native to Europe, central Russia and western Asia. Stiff, grooved, hollow stems have branches rising at a steep angle and grow up to 75 cm high. Lower **leaves** at the base form a rosette near the ground.

The stalked lower leaves may be toothed or deeply divided into triangular lobes. Rough, hairy upper leaves clasp the stem. **Flower** heads are borne in clusters of two or three in the angles of the upper leaves and stems from summer to autumn. The sky-blue flowers are made up of rays of strap-shaped petals and are about 3–5 cm wide. Flowers usually open only in the mornings. Chicory can be found naturalised in open pasture, roadsides and waste areas throughout the country and can become quite weedy in some areas. The taproot has long been roasted and used as a coffee substitute and the leaves can be used in salads.

Family Scrophulariaceae. A Southern European evergreen perennial growing to 6 cm high and spreading over 50 cm wide. This trailing plant is hairless and has alternate, pale to mid-green, kidney to round-shaped **leaves** that have five to nine rounded lobes. Leaves look similar to ivy leaves. Successions of tiny lilac to pale purple **flowers** with yellow throats are 9–15 mm long and are borne on slender stalks. Each flower has a short spur, giving it the appearance of a snapdragon flower. Flowering is from spring to late summer and often through the winter in mild climates. Plants can be found naturalising in shady rocks, cliff faces or walls where the roots can get a grip in sparse soil. This species is ultra-hardy and can be invasive. *Cymbalaria* comes from Latin 'cymbalum' meaning cymbal, referring to the rounded leaf shape. *Muralis* means 'growing on walls'.

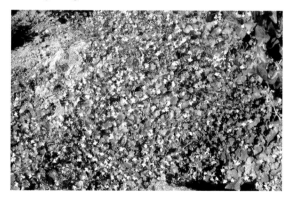

Chinese forget-me-not *Cynoglossum amabile*

Family Boraginaceae. This is a biennial in its original habitat in south-western China, but usually is treated as an annual. It has an upright, branching habit, growing 45–60 cm tall and 30 cm wide. **Leaves** are oblong to lanceolate with a greyish down of silky hairs. **Flowers** are arranged in 6 cm-wide terminal sprays and are

around 5 mm across and slightly funnel-shaped. They are usually turquoise-blue but pink and white forms are also commonly found. The **seeds** are covered with barbed bristles, which stick to clothing and animal fur, hence the common name of forget-me-not.

Cynoglossum thrive in sunny or slightly shaded open ground in home gardens where they bloom in spring or early summer and then seed down profusely. The genus name *Cynoglossum* is derived from Greek words for 'dog' and 'tongue', hence its other common name of Chinese hound's tongue. This species should not be confused with the *Myosotis* species that are also commonly called forget-me-nots.

Family Scrophulariaceae. Originating in Western Europe, the foxglove is a biennial plant with soft, hairy, toothed, ovate to lance-olate **leaves** in a basal rosette, 20–30 cm across. The life span of the plant is two seasons. In the first year growth remains in a basal rosette of leaves. Second-year growth produces flowering stems, 90 cm in height. One-sided spikes have purple-to-white-spotted, thimble-like **flowers** that hang down and last about six days. Fox-gloves roam the land of New Zealand, finding homes in pastures, roadsides and waste areas where farmers often regard them as a noxious weed. The earliest known name for this plant is the Anglo-Saxon 'foxes glofa', the glove of the fox. It derives this name from the flowers, which resemble the fingers of a glove, and possibly from a northern legend that bad fairies gave the blossoms to the fox to put on his toes, so that he might soften his tread while he hunted for prey. Ingestion of this plant can be fatal at any time during the life of the plant; it is most toxic just before the seeds ripen. Digitalis is used commercially as a cardiac drug.

Viper's bugloss *Echium vulgare*

Family Boraginaceae. Native to Europe, this is an upright annual or biennial plant growing to around 60–90 cm high. It is a rough plant covered in a mass of stiff, whitish **hairs**. The alternate **leaves** are sessile, lanceolate, a dark green and can reach up to 25 cm in length. The leaves can be as wide as 3 cm and progressively become smaller up the stems. The **flowers** are in numerous dense spikes, funnel-shaped with unequal lobes and protruding stamens. They are up to 2 cm wide, pink in the bud and bright blue when open. Long, slender sepals conceal the **fruit** that consists of four nutlets that look rather like a snake's head. Blooms first appear in early summer and continue into mid-autumn. Plants can be found in dry, open fields, roadsides and waste areas where it can form vast colonies. The plant was traditionally used for curing snakebites, hence its common name.

Bugloss comes from the Greek word for ox tongue, referring to the rough, tongue-shaped leaves. *E. plantagineum*, Paterson's curse, is also commonly found, mostly in dry areas in the North Island. Although this plant is sometimes considered a weed in Australia, it is not so troublesome here. It is a similar plant to *E. vulgare* but has larger flowers. Both plants are very attractive to bees and are used for honey production.

Family Brassicaceae. This is an upright biennial or short-lived perennial native to Europe and western Asia. Typically the plant will grow 60–90 cm tall and 30–60 cm across. The multi-branched stems carry dark green, alternate, lanceolate, sessile **leaves** up 12 cm long. Large spikes of showy white, lavender or purple **flowers** are in loose, terminal racemes. Each flower is cross-shaped, up to 2 cm across with four oblong petals. The

flowers are very fragrant, particularly in the evening, and flowering is from spring to summer. Plants can be found mostly in home gardens but also in parks and reserves. It is an invasive weed that threatens native plant habitats in some countries but has not really escaped from cultivation or caused problems in New Zealand. Dame's rocket is one of the showiest members of the Brassicaceae family. It is sometimes confused with phlox but its flowers have four petals, while phloxes all have five petals. Plants are also commonly called sweet rocket or dame's violet. *Hesperis* possibly comes from the Greek word 'hesperos' for 'west' or 'evening', referring to the tendency for the fragrance to increase in the evening, and *matronalis* meaning 'of married women'. The Roman matronal festival coincided with its blooming each spring.

English bluebell *Hyacinthoides non-scripta*

Family Hyacinthaceae. Native to Western Europe, including Great Britain, the English bluebell is a woodland bulb growing around 30 cm high. **Leaves** are long, strap-shaped, deep green, upright at first then spreading or flattening after flowering. Blue, bell-shaped **flowers**, up to 2 cm long, are borne in clusters in vertical layers along single stalks. The tube of the flower is short with tips curled backwards. Bracts at the base of the flower stalk are the same colour as the flower. Although called bluebells, pink and white forms can also be found. Flowering is in spring and plants can be found throughout the country naturalising in home gardens, parks, reserves and waste ground, mostly in shady woodland areas. This flower has been grown in European gardens since 1500; a synonym is

Scilla non-scripta. Spanish bluebell, *Hyacinthoides hispanica*, is also commonly found. It has similar characteristics with lots of broad, bell-shaped flowers hanging from sturdy, round flower stalks and grows 40–50 cm high. It is more robust and flowers slightly later than its English cousin.

Japanese iris *Iris japonica*

Family Iridaceae. This plant was introduced from China to Japan in ancient times. It is an evergreen perennial with creeping aerial **rhizomes** rooting at intervals and growing 30–70 cm high. The **leaves** are strap-shaped, 30–80 cm long, 2–5 cm wide, mid-green, glossy and form a broad fan from the base of the plant. Branched stems support many **flowers** that open in succession, blooming in the morning and shrivelling in the evening. Flowers are white to pale blue or purplish, 5–6 cm across. Each flower is spotted with a deeper lilac shade. A yellow, lineal crest, rather like a cockscomb,

is prominent on the petal falls. Flowering is in spring and plants can be found naturalising in shady woodland areas, mostly in home gardens, parks and reserves throughout the country, but it is somewhat frost tender. This is a member of the crested iris family: the crested iris has a raised ridge on the falls, whereas the bearded iris has a beard on the falls. *Iris* is named for the Greek goddess of the rainbow; *japonica* means 'of Japan or China'.

Purple linaria *Linaria purpurea*

Family Scrophulariaceae. Originating in southern Italy and Sicily this linaria is an upright perennial growing 60–90 cm high and 30–40 cm wide. It has linear, grey to mid-green **leaves**, which change from being whorled to alternate as they go up the stem.

Slender spikes carrying small violet-blue **flowers**, snapdragon-like and 1–2 cm long, with two lips and a curved spur at the base of the petals, are produced in a dense, terminal raceme. Flowering is in summer followed by prolific seeding in the autumn. Plants can be found mostly in home gardens, parks and waste areas throughout the country where it quickly naturalises to form large clumps. Dry, stony railway and road embankments are also a common habitat. Other common names are purple toadflax and perennial snapdragon. There are a number of commonly found hybrids in pink, white and purple that easily naturalise as well. *Linaria vulgaris*, butter and eggs, has petals that are bright to cream-yellow with a dull orange centre. It grows about the same height but reproduces from rhizomes as well as seeds. *Linaria* is for the leaves' resemblance to those of *Linum* (flax).

Family Linaceae. A European native perennial herb that has up to a dozen close-growing stems arising 60 cm high from a somewhat woody base with a long taproot. The densely leafy stems produce numerous small, narrowly lanceolate, single-veined and stalkless grey-green **leaves**, 6–12 mm long. Dozens of bright blue **flowers**, 15–30 mm across, occur in drooping clusters at the tip of each stem. The saucer-shaped flowers have five petals that fall shortly after opening. Blue flax flowers in summer and grows in dry and stony places, mostly in home gardens. For many years, blue flax was called Lewis' flax in honour of Captain Meriwether Lewis of the Lewis and Clark Expedition. Members of the expedition first discovered the plant in Montana, United States but botanists have since ascertained that the plant is a variety of a species long grown in Europe as an ornamental. *Perenne* means 'lasting the whole year'. The stiff stems on this species show why its relative *Linum usitatissimum* is used to make flax for cloth and linen.

Family Cruciferae/Brassicaceae. This biennial plant is a native of south-east Europe. In the first year a dense rosette of large, toothed, heart-shaped, hairy, green **leaves** develops. In the second year a stout, leafy, loosely branched flower stem grows up to 1 m high with a 30–40 cm spread. In spring the flower stem is topped with elongated clusters of 12 mm-wide, cross-shaped **flowers**. The lightly fragrant flowers are usually reddish-purple but white forms are sometimes found. Blooms are followed by flat, circular **seedpods** that are called silicles. When ripe the green outer covering peels off to reveal a silvery, papery septum and winged seeds. These translucent, silvery pods are used for indoor decoration and their resemblance to silver dollars has also given this plant another common name, the money plant. Plants can be found in sunny or part shady areas in home gardens and waste areas where it quickly naturalises. The name *Lunaria* comes from the moon-like appearance of the ripe seedpods.

Virginia stock *Malcomia maritima*

Family Cruciferae/Brassicaceae. This is a slender, erect, fast-growing annual, native to the Mediterranean region. It will grow 15–20 cm high with a 10 cm spread and has blunt, elliptic, grey-green **leaves**. Flowering can begin just four weeks after seed germination. The plant will rapidly become covered in four-petalled, 1–2 cm **flowers** in shades from white to pink, lilac and

magenta, and has the general appearance of garden stocks, *Matthiola*, in miniature. The cross-shaped flowers are carried on slender stems and are sweetly scented. Flowering will occur in spring to early summer and cease with hot weather. This plant is usually found colonising sunny or sandy places in home gardens and is a traditional edging plant for flowerbeds and borders. Virginia stock was one of the many plants whose name was dedicated to the Virgin Mary and was known as the Virgin stock. After the Reformation many of the plants that had previously been dedicated to the Virgin had their names changed again in such a way as to refer to any girl or woman, rather than to a specific one.

Chatham Island forget-me-not *Myosotidium hortensia*

Family Boraginaceae. This is a genus of just one plant that occurs naturally only on the Chatham Islands of New Zealand. It is a herbaceous, clump-forming perennial growing 50–60 cm tall and wide and is dormant in winter in colder districts. Huge glossy, bright green, veined, kidney-shaped **leaves**, 25–40 cm wide, help make this plant truly spectacular. Large, rounded **flower** heads up to 15 cm wide are formed on strong stems that rise above the foliage. Each flower head has a dense mass of small, forget-me-not style flowers, 2–3 cm across, of an intense sky-blue with white margins. Flowering is in spring and plants can be found in damp, shaded, woodland-type gardens, parks and reserves. In its natural habitat it thrives near the coast.

Forget-me-not *Myosotis sylvatica*

Family Boraginaceae. A familiar species from most of Europe. This biennial plant is bushy and is covered with short hairs on branching stems to 30 cm high. The mid-green, oblong-lanceolate **leaves** are also hairy. Tiny, fragrant, sky-blue **flowers** have a

yellow eye when fresh. They are up to 2 cm wide and are classic forget-me-not style. The flowers are carried on open sprays and herald the first signs of spring, flowering right through to summer. The plant likes a rich, moist soil in part shade and it can be commonly found growing in waste areas and roadsides as well as home gardens. A susceptibility to powdery mildew often means the plant can look untidy and straggly in the summer before it sets seed and dies off. This species can be confused with the Chinese forget-me-not, *Cynoglossum amabile*, which has similar flowers but a very different growth habit. Forget-me-nots have long been a symbol of loving remembrance. Romantic legends have followed this tiny flower through the ages. From as early as the 1st century until the 17th century, forget-me-not was also considered a medicinal plant, useful for healing bites and stings. The flower appeared in the pleasure gardens of the 18th century and reached the height of its popularity a century later.

Baby blue eyes *Nemophila menziesii*

Family Hydrophyllacaea. From a genus of 13 species of hardy annuals, baby blue eyes is native to California, United States. Sprawling mounds of slender, trailing stems grow to a height and spread of 15–20 cm. The stems carry feathery, deeply cut, light-green pinnate **leaves** and a profusion of white-centred, sky-blue **flowers**. The flower, 2–3 cm wide, is saucer-shaped with five

Nemophila maculata.

rounded, overlapping petals and prominent veins. The beautiful sky-blue colour fades slightly as the flower ages. Flowering is usually in spring but can extend into summer. The plant can be found mostly in home gardens where it will colonise border edges but does best in light shade, as the genus name suggests: *nemos* is Greek for woodland and *philos* means lover. The name *menziesii* is from Archibald Menzies, a Scottish botanist and surgeon on the expedition of the ship *Discovery* that visited California 1792–94. *Nemophila maculata* is from the same clan with similar growth habit but has white flowers with purple veins and a prominent purple blotch on the tip of each petal, thus its common name of five spot.

Love in a mist *Nigella damascena*

Family Ranunculaceae. A native of the Mediterranean region, this is a fast-growing, hardy annual plant that forms bushy mounds of slender stems to around 60 cm high and 20–30 cm wide. Erect stems carry bright green, finely cut, ferny **leaves**. Showy blue **flowers** are surrounded by a cloud of light green, lacy, finely divided leaf-like bracts and resemble cornflowers, *Centaurea*, in shape and colour. Each flower is around 3–5 cm across and can be single or double in form. After flowering, each blossom becomes a balloon-like green **seedpod**, 5–6 cm long and striped with purple or bronze. The attractive seedpods are popular for dried arrangements. Flowering is in spring to summer and plants can be found naturalising mostly in home gardens. Pink and white-coloured flowers are also commonly found. The unusual common name, love in a mist, refers to the way the flowers appear through the 'nest' of thread-like bracts. The flower's genus name is from the Latin 'niger', meaning black, which refers to the colour of its **seeds**. Cut flowers are long-lasting if the foliage from the lower part of the stem is removed.

Family Fabaceae. A ground-hugging, perennial plant that grows to a height of 10 cm and can spread out to 1 m in width. It is native to the Himalayas, East India and East Africa. The bright green, 2–3 cm **leaves** have a distinctive arc of maroon that circles the lobes and are trifoliate (clover-like), hence the name shamrock. The **flowers**, 1–2 cm wide, characteristically pea-flower-shaped, are of a vivid blue colour and flower in summer and autumn. *Parochetus* is a good ground-covering species that colonises robustly in both shady and sunny situations, especially waste ground. It is often found naturalising in parks, reserves and private gardens under evergreen trees and shrubs where it will take root as it spreads out. The plant is nearly deciduous in winter. Shamrock is the English form of the Irish word 'seamrog', which literally translated means 'little clover' or 'young clover'.

Purple tansy *Phacelia tanacetifolia*

Family Hydrophyllaceae. An annual, native to south-western United States and Mexico, growing around 80 cm high but sometimes up to 120 cm. Stems are hairy and erect with multiple branches. **Leaves** are 5–10 cm long, pinnate and finely cut. Lilac or mauve **flowers** are in single or branched, crowded cymes at the end of tall **spikes**. Each flower is around 1 cm wide, slightly cup-shaped, and has long stamens radiating outwards. Both the leaves and the flowers give the whole plant a lacy appearance and flowering is in spring and summer. Plants can be found in home gardens, meadow gardens and sometimes along roadsides. This plant is used extensively throughout the world to attract beneficial insects as it has a good pollen source for attracting syrphids, members of the fly family. The name *Phacelia* is based on the Greek 'phakelos', cluster, alluding to the densely crowded flower spikes of most species of the genus. *Tanacetifolia* means tansy-leaved, with leaves like the species *Tanacetum*. Another common name is lacy phacelia.

Senecio skirrhodon.

Family Asteraceae. From a large genus of some 3000 species this is an annual plant native to South Africa. It has an upright habit growing to 60 cm high. The **leaves** are quite large and variable, dark green, oblong to ovate, usually deeply pinnately lobed and have a clammy feel. The purple, sometimes pink, daisy **flowers**, 3–4 cm across, are carried in clusters at the top of the stems. The flower has a central disc that is bright yellow, full of pollen and nectar that attracts bees and beetles. Once pollinated the flower head turns into a fluffy white ball, ready for the wind to disperse the **seeds**. Flowering is in spring. This *Senecio* can be quite weedy and plants can be found naturalising in dry, sandy coastal areas, sand dunes, waste areas and home gardens. *Senecio skirrhodon*, gravel groundsel, is another annual, sometimes perennial, that forms a mound 40–60 cm high. Leaves are light green and spear-shaped with clusters of yellow flowers, 2–3 cm across, in summer. It is found in coastal areas and waste places, often helping to stabilise sand dunes. *Senecio* comes from 'senex' meaning 'old man', referring to the grey hairs on the seeds.

Purple top *Verbena bonariensis*

Family Verbenaceae. Purple top is an erect, clump-forming perennial native to South America. It has stiff, widely branched, square stems with bristly hairs on the angles. It can reach 1–1.8 m in height with an open, airy spread of 30–90 cm. **Leaves** are lanceolate to oblong-lanceolate in shape and mid-green in colour. Most of the leaves are clustered in a mounded rosette at the base of the plant. The relatively scarce stem leaves are opposite, 7–13 cm long and clasp the stems. The **flowers** are lilac-purple, 5 mm across, and borne in tightly packed cymes about 5–8 cm wide. The centre flower in the cluster opens first and later-opening flowers are on the ends of lateral branches that arise from below the first flower. Flowering is all summer long, until the first frost of

autumn. This plant is sometimes grown in gardens as an ornamental but is more often considered a weed along roadsides, waste areas and pastures. *Bonariensis* is Latin for Buenos Aires.

33

Greater periwinkle *Vinca major*

Family Apocynaceae. *Vinca major* is an evergreen trailing groundcover native to Europe. It will grow 30 cm high and spread rapidly with stems up to 2 m long, rooting at the tip of the stem. The plant will form a mat that can colonise large areas. The glossy **leaves** are ovate, opposite, mid to dark green and 2–9 cm long. Purplish-blue **flowers** have a white ring around the centre and five distinctively square-cut petals. Flowers are solitary, 3–5 cm across and grow from the leaf axils. Flowering is nearly all year around and plants can be found in both sunny and shaded waste ground areas, roadsides and banks. *Vinca minor*, lesser periwinkle, is similar but has a smaller leaf and flower and roots at the nodes along the stems. A variegated foliage form is also commonly found. Children often pull the petals off the periwinkle flower to leave the flower style that looks like a fairy wand. The plant has historically been used to treat a wide assortment of diseases.

Wild pansy *Viola tricolor*

Family Violaceae. This European native is an annual, some-times a perennial, clump-forming plant, often with spreading stems. It grows 10–30 cm high and around 10–20 cm wide. Stems are upright, branching, hollow and covered by short hairs. The mid-green **leaves** are alternate, ovate to lanceolate with rounded teeth. At the foot of the leaf stalk there are deeply lobed, leaf-like stip-ules. The typical pansy-like **flowers** are 1–2 cm across and appear on long stems in the leaf axils. Colours vary from cream and yellow to dark blue and purple-black, often with two or three colours. The **seed** capsule splits into three parts, dries and cracks, scattering the seeds large distances, hence another common name, Johnny jump ups. Flowering is from spring to autumn and plants can be found mostly naturalising in home gar-dens, parks and reserves. The pansy has long been associated with love, accounting for the folk name, heartsease. Many common garden pansies are derived from this plant, mostly due to its ability to produce various colours in one flower. It also has some medicinal properties.

35

Family Gentianaceae. Native to most of Europe, centaury is a variable biennial species. It is low-growing to around 50 cm, hairless and forms a basal rosette. Basal **leaves** are ovate to elliptical; stem leaves smaller and narrower. Flat-topped heads have numerous starry bright pink

flowers, 1–2 cm across, with the flower bracts longer than the sepals. Flowering is in late spring through to late summer. Centaury is an attractive, common weed of open waste areas and roadsides and can be found throughout the country. It has long been associated with medicinal use, hence its other common names, feverwort or bitter herb. Historically, centaury was recommended and used for practically every complaint. The herbalist Culpepper wrote that: 'the herbe is so safe that you cannot fail in the using of it, only give it inwardly for inward diseases, use it outwardly for outward diseases. Tis very wholesome, but not very toothsome'. The name is derived from a legend that a Greek warrior, when wounded by a poisoned arrow, cured himself with centaury.

Red valerian *Centranthus ruber*

Family Valerianaceae. Of European origin, valerian is a herbaceous perennial growing 60–90 cm high. It has an upright habit with stems branching from the base of the plant. The **leaves** are long oval to lance-shaped, opposite paired, and the upper leaves are stalkless on the stem and slightly toothed. The leaves emit an unpleasant smell when crushed. Panicles of fragrant **flowers** are borne on rounded terminal heads. Flowers are red or deep pink, star-shaped, 1 cm across, each having a single stamen. A short, slender spur extends back from the base of the flower, which is why it is also sometimes called spur valerian. Flowering is from late spring to late autumn. Plants can be found colonising banks, walls, roadsides and even cliff faces. Young leaves can be eaten in salads or as cooked greens

and the roots used in soups. Do not confuse this plant with the true medicinal valerian, *Valeriana officinalis*; it does not have the same medicinal value. Centranthus comes from the Greek words 'kentron', a spur, and 'anthos', flower, referring to the flower having a spur-like base. *Ruber* is Latin for 'red'.

Farewell to spring *Clarkia amoena*

Family Onagraceae. Aptly named, as this is one of the last spring annuals to come into flower. This upright and bushy plant grows 30–60 cm high and is native to north-west California in the United States. The **leaves** are lanceolate, 1–6 cm long and deep green in colour. Cup-shaped, four-petalled **flowers** sit in clusters on top of tall, thin stems. The flower petals are satiny, obo-vate to fan-shaped, 1–3 cm long, and come in a range of pink to lavender shades with dark pink blotches. Flowering is followed by tapering **seedpods** filled with many small brown seeds. Farewell to spring can be found in open, sunny situations in private gardens, parks, reserves and meadow gardens. It grows quickly, blooms heavily from late spring to mid-summer and then dies with frost. This plant is often called godetia, but usually this name will refer to cultivars rather than the true wildflower. The original wildflower is often thought to be more beautiful than all the hybrids that have been created from it.

Native ice plant *Disphyma australe*

Family Aizoaceae. This plant is the most common one of two species native to New Zealand. It is a mat-forming, creeping succulent growing around 10 cm high and rooting at the nodes. The stems can reach up to 60 cm long. The shiny **leaves** are thick and fleshy, 3–6 cm long, triangular in section and united at the base. Flower stems are short and thick  with solitary pink or white, daisy-like **flower** heads. The flower is around 3 cm wide with 50–60 petals. Flowering is from spring to autumn. Small, rounded **fruits** are produced continuously following flowering. Plants can be found clothing cliffs and rocks in coastal areas in both the North and South Islands where it can form large carpets or hanging curtains. Plants are also grown in parks, reserves and home gardens. Ice plants are so called because of their crystalline leaf tissues. The thickened leaves and stems store water, allowing the plant to grow in dry and salty areas. The Maori name is horokaka and it is synonymous with *Mesembryanthemum australe*.

Shore spurge *Euphorbia glauca*

Family Euphorbiaceae. Shore spurge is a coastal plant endemic to New Zealand, the Chatham Islands and Norfolk Island. From a genus of over 2000 species this is the only New Zealand native. The plant has a slightly creeping habit with new, erect, reddish stems coming up from underground rhizomes to form a clump 60–100 cm tall. The alternate, oblanceolate **leaves** are waxy, bluish-green and glaucous. They are 8–10 cm long and become smaller and more crowded towards the top of the stems. **Flower** heads are in terminal bunches with contrasting maroon bracts surrounding the tiny, red 5–10 mm flowers. Flowering is in spring and summer. This plant can be found on coastal cliffs, sand dunes and rocky lake shores. It is a threatened plant in its natural habitat but is increasingly used for coastal dune control and commercial landscaping as it is particularly suited to dry or loose soils. This plant is also commonly called sand spurge.

Cranesbill *Geranium maderense*

Family Geraniaceae. A biennial, sometimes a perennial, native to Madeira and the Canary Islands, this is probably the largest of all geraniums. It will grow up to 1.2 m high and develops quickly into a large mound with large **leaves** on radiating stems. As the plant grows the older stems bend down to the ground, making an architectural support system. The stems are wine red in colour and very showy. The light green leaves are deeply divided into five segments, each twice-lobed and toothed. The flowering stems and sepals are all covered with purple hairs that catch the light and decorate the plant. Even after flowering, when the plant is declining, these hairs are attractive for several weeks. In the second or third year of growth huge, hazy sprays of **flowers** measuring up to 1 m across are produced. Each flower is magenta-pink with a dark eye and central stripes on the petals. The flower is 2–3 cm across and has five petals. Flowering is for about six weeks in spring. Plants can be found naturalising in home gardens, parks and reserves in more temperate climate areas. This plant is somewhat like an overgrown herb Robert, *Geranium robertianum*, and a similarly invasive seeder.

Herb Robert *Geranium robertianum*

Family Geraniaceae. This is an annual or semi-evergreen perennial growing in clumps about 30 cm high and wide. Foliage is
deeply dissected with the **leaves** and stems being covered in fine
hairs. Stems branch from the base with some being upright and
some sprawling. Leaves are palmately cut into three to five deeply
lobed leaflets. They are bright green with a reddish tinge that
becomes bright red to bronze in the autumn. The stems are bright
red. **Flowers** usually occur in pairs with hairy sepals similar to the
leaves and stems. Flowers have five petals, 10 stamens and one
style and are bright pink, occasionally white and 10–15 mm
across. Both stems and foliage have a strong and unpleasant odour
if the leaves are crushed or if clumps are dug up. It doesn't smell
if left undisturbed. Since herb Robert blooms and seeds from
spring to autumn it can become invasive. It prefers shady, moist
areas and is widely distributed along roadsides, wastelands and
home gardens. Herb Robert has well over 100 names in England
alone with many folklore associations.

Family Balsaminaceae. Originating from the Himalayas, this is a robust, erect and branching annual which can reach well over 1 m in one season with a 60 cm spread. The upright, hollow stems are easily broken and they have a purplish tinge. **Leaves** are smooth and hairless, narrowly ovate and 6–20 cm long. The leaf margins are sharply serrated with 20 teeth or more along each side. Each leaf has a short, stout stem. The helmet-like, white to pink or purple **flowers**, 3–4 cm long, are produced in racemes in the leaf axils. Fused sepals form a spur on each flower. Flowering is from spring until summer. The **fruit** is a five-chambered capsule that explodes at the slightest touch and ejects up to 800 seeds. This plant can become invasive if allowed to spread and can be found growing in moist, shady gardens, roadsides and waste areas in warmer parts of the country, especially moist riverbanks. All parts of the plant emit an unpleasant odour when touched. This species is sometimes also known as policeman's helmet.

Red hot poker *Kniphofia uvaria*

Family Liliaceae. From a genus of about 75 species native to South Africa *Kniphofia uvaria* is the most commonly found species in New Zealand. It is a robust herbaceous perennial with coarse, hollow to sub-hollow, mid-green, linear **leaves** forming clumps from a thickened root crown and spreading to about 60 cm wide. Smooth flower stems, 1 m or more high, rise erectly above the foliage to terminate in poker-like spikes. Each spike has close-ly set tubular **flowers**, 3–4 cm long, with open ends pointing obliquely downwards. The bright scarlet-red flowers are well deserved of the 'red hot poker' name; they are fire-red on the tips cooling to yellow moving down the stem. This plant has been a national summer to autumn-flowering favourite for decades, where it is commonly found at the farm verge, gate or down the drive. Plants will thrive in areas with stiff competition from road-side grasses. *Kniphofia* is named after Johann Hieronymus Kniphof (1704–63), a professor of medicine and author of a work of botanical illustrations.

Everlasting pea *Lathyrus latifolius*

Family Fabaceae. Native to Europe, this is a climbing perennial similar to the garden sweet peas. The plant will climb up to 2 m each year and it can also sprawl or tumble down banks. It is virtually evergreen in warm climates. The multiple stems branch from the base and are heavily winged and hairless. **Leaves** are alternate, pinnate with two linear to lanceolate leaflets and have branched, terminal tendrils. Racemes of 5–20 **flowers** are usually rose-purple, sometimes white, mottled pink or pink with dark veins. Each flower is around 2–3 cm long and typically pea-shaped. Flowering is in profusion all summer long and plants can be found naturalising in waste places, banks, roadsides and coastal sands as well as home gardens. This plant is also commonly named the perennial pea and has been in cultivation since the early 1700s. This pea has naturalised nearly worldwide, having escaped from early Victorian gardens. *Lathyrus* is from the Greek 'lathyros', an old name for 'pea'. The common garden variety is an annual, *L. odoratus*.

Scarlet flax *Linum grandiflorum rubrum*

Family Linaceae. The genus *Linum* comprises about 90 species. The scarlet flax is an annual, growing up to 60 cm and native to North Africa and Southern Europe. Singular, upright, stiff stems support open clusters of flowering stems forming in the leaf axils and concentrated in the upper part of the plant. Flowering stems are around 20 cm long. **Leaves** are light green, lanceolate, alternate with prominent veins and about 4 cm long on the main stem and 2 cm long on the flowering stems. Brilliant crimson-red **flowers** are slightly cup-shaped, 3 cm wide and have five overlapping petals. Each flower has a satiny sheen, a dark red centre and dark red petal tips. Flowers bloom in profusion, although each flower lasts only one day and will close up at night. Flowering is in spring to early summer, finishing before the heat of summer. Scarlet flax can be found mostly in home gardens and wildflower meadows and is sought after for its shimmering and airy beauty.

Family Caryophyllaceae. Rose campion is a clump-forming perennial, sometimes biennial, plant of south-east Europe, widely cultivated for its attractive woolly foliage and showy flowers. The plant will grow 60–75 cm high and spread 30–45 cm. Basal clumps have ovate to lanceolate, densely woolly, 8–10 cm, silver-grey **leaves**. The leaves of the flowering stems are much smaller than the basal leaves. Bright rose-magenta, 3 cm-wide, five-petalled **flowers** are borne in open clusters on woolly stems. Flowering is from spring through to summer followed by 1 cm-long **seed capsules** with five prominent ribs. When the seed is developed the capsules dry and open at the top like little jars. This plant can be found mostly in home gardens, parks, reserves and waste areas. It is a prolific self-seeder and will naturalise in warm, sunny areas. There are two meanings of the word *Lychnis*, both from the Greek for 'lamp'. One refers to the flame-coloured flowers of some species and the other alludes to the ancient use of the felt-like leaves as lamp wicks. A white-flowered form, *Lychnis coronaria alba*, is also commonly found.

Purple loosestrife *Lythrum salicaria*

Family Lythraceae. A herbaceous perennial of Eurasian origin growing to 1.8 m tall. Stout, erect stems are covered with fine hairs, square in section and with a rib at each corner. The plant usually has a single stem but sometimes may have a few short branches.

Leaves are mid-green, ovate to narrowly lanceolate and stalkless. The lower leaves are in whorls of three and the upper leaves are in opposite pairs. **Flowers** are in whorls of six set in the angle between the stem and the small leaf-like bracts and packed on 30 cm-long spires. The flower is pinkish-purple in colour, has 12 stamens and six petals, 10 mm long, lance-shaped with darker veins. Flowering is in spring and summer with plants being found mostly in country gardens or waste wetlands such as marshes, lakesides and riverbanks. Although a very attractive plant it can become invasive in wetlands. The juice of the plant is rich in tannins and has been used as an alternative to oak bark for tanning leather.

Common mallow *Malva sylvestris*

Family Malvaceae. Common mallow is a biennial or short-lived perennial originating from most of Europe, Africa and Asia. Plants have upright or trailing stems that grow around 90 cm high and around 30 cm wide. The dark-green basal **leaves** are palmately divided with three to seven rounded and toothed lobes. The stem leaves are smaller and more

deeply divided. Showy, rosy-purple **flowers** come in clusters of two or more, 2–5 cm wide, in the axils of the leaves. The flower has five petals with dark veins and is spirally twisted in the bud. **Fruits** are a circle of single-seeded segments or nutlets, 1 cm across, with an appearance rather like a small round cheese. Mallow will begin blooming in mid-summer and continue flowering until frost and can be found throughout the country in pastures, waste ground, roadsides and sometimes on coastal rocks and sand dunes. Although quite attractive, this plant can be invasive. It is also commonly known as large-flowered mallow but some folk names refer to the ring of nutlets: Billy buttons, pancake plant and cheese flower are examples. Mallow has been used medicinally and as a vegetable. *Malva* is Latin for 'mallow', from the Greek 'malakos', referring to the leaves and an ointment made from the seeds, which was supposed to be soothing to the skin.

49

Long-headed poppy *Papaver dubium*

Family Papaveraceae. An annual plant, native to Europe, growing to around 60 cm high. It has an erect habit with a basal rosette of **leaves** that die as the plant matures. The stems are branched and covered with tightly pressed hairs. The mid-green leaves are up to 20 cm long, deeply lobed or pinnately divided into broad, spear-shaped segments that are 5–10 cm wide and covered with hairs. The **flowers** are borne at the end of long stems covered with hairs. Flowers are usually up to 5 cm in diameter with four orange-

red and unblotched petals, which usually only persist for a single day. The broad, overlapping petals taper towards the base to form a characteristic cup or bowl shape. The hairless **seed capsule** is elongated and narrow, up to 2.5 cm long. If the stem or leaves are broken a white latex is exuded. Flowering is in spring and summer and plants can be found naturalising mostly in the South Island along roadsides, in dry pastures and waste areas. This plant is similar to *Papaver rhoeas*, the soldier poppy, but is smaller in habit and the hairs are pressed against the stems rather than spreading out from it. The flowers are paler without any dark blotches.

Soldier poppy *Papaver rhoeas*

Family Papaveraceae. Hairy, upright, branched stems grow to about 1 m high on this annual, red poppy from Europe and North Africa. The **leaves** are coarsely toothed, hairy and pinnately lobed. If cut the stems exude a milky-white latex. Large, scarlet **flowers** are 6–10 cm across, often with a dark blotch at the petal base. Four thin, delicate, crumpled petals contain numerous purplish-black stamens and a rounded, flat-topped ovary. The **seedpods** are rounded and flat-topped. This popular wildflower will flower from early to late summer and has a timeless history of both home garden and field cultivation; in fact it is considered internationally the most popular wild-flower of all. The soldier poppy can be found in both home

gardens and cultivated meadow gardens. It will flourish on waste ground but soil must be cultivated occasionally for the seeds to germinate. Poppy seeds have been known to germinate after being buried for 50–100 years, when the soil is disturbed. Each plant of a poppy is believed to produce anything from 20,000 to 50,000 seeds! After the First World War the scarlet field poppy growing in the fields near Flanders became more important than any other wildflower in history. It was first the flower of consolation and later became the emblem of remembrance.

51

Corn poppy *Papaver rhoeas*

Family Papaveraceae. Similar to the soldier poppy and originating from England, this annual plant forms ferny clumps with hairy, upright stems up to 90 cm high. The blue/green **leaves** are coarsely toothed, hairy and pinnately lobed. Large, 6–10 cm,

single **flowers** exhibit colour shades of white, rose-pink, salmon and white-edged pink. Unlike the soldier poppy there is no black spot on the flowers and the stamens are characteristically yellow or white. Flowering is from spring to early summer. The corn poppy can be found in open, wasteland areas as well as in home gardens and it is a major component of cultivated meadow gardens. The **seed-pods** are rounded and flat-topped. Pale-coloured poppies had been grown in 17th-century gardens but these had all but disappeared until around 1880 a Reverend Wilks in the town of Shirley, England rediscovered a wild plant. Repeated seed selection produced what has become known as Shirley poppies. Corn poppies were once a common weed of the English cornfields but modern farming techniques have mostly eliminated them today.

New Zealand flax *Phormium tenax*

Family Liliacae. A native New Zealand, clump-forming plant from a genus of two species. The plant has stiff, erect, coarse **leaves** up to 3 m long and 5–12 cm wide. The colour can vary from light yellow-green to deep blue-green. Flower stalks can reach up to 5 m high with **flowers** in large panicles. Each flower is around 2.5 cm long, brownish-red and with stamens longer than the petals. Flowering is in late spring and summer and plants can be found from lowland and coastal swamps to low mountain areas throughout the country. The Maori name is harakeke. The other New Zealand species, *Phormium cookianum*, mountain flax or wharariki, generally has drooping leaves up to 1.5 m long and flower stalks up to 2 m. Many side stems carry yellowish-orange flowers and a drooping, twisted seed head. It is found from sea level to subalpine cliffs. Both species have been extensively cultivated and these, along with many hybrids, are very common, forming a distinctive part of our landscape. The leaves are extremely strong and have been of great importance to Maori for weaving into decorative, clothing and household items.

Pink head knotweed *Polygonum capitatum*

Family Polygonaceae. This perennial, evergreen plant is from the warm, temperate areas of the Himalayas. It is a very vigorous trailing groundcover, growing around 15 cm high. **Leaves** are 1–5 cm

long, ovate, deep green with a burgundy V-shape pointing towards the leaf tip. The stems, undersides of leaves, leaf midribs and edges all have a reddish colour. Distinctive **flower** heads are like tiny pink balls, 1–2 cm across, at the tip of each stem. Flowers are very numerous, lasting almost all the year round. The plant favours dry banks, roadside banks and waste areas in full sun, forming a strong mat in warm, temperate areas of the country. This plant can become quite invasive. It is also sometimes called smartweed. *Polygonum* means 'many knee-joints', because of the thickened joints on the stem.

Sweet briar *Rosa rubiginosa*

Family Rosaceae. Sweet briar is a deciduous, European shrub, 1–3 m tall, consisting of woody stems or canes with unequal hooked prickles or spines. Canes arise from a crown, supported by extensive shallow roots that shoot at the nodes. The **leaves** have between two and four pairs of typically rose-shaped, oval, toothed leaflets with many sticky fruity-scented glands on the undersurface. The fruity scent of the leaves when rubbed is quite strong and distinctive. The clear-pink, five-petalled **flowers** are 5–6 cm across and also have a pleasant fragrance. These flowers decorate the branches in summer and are followed by long-lasting, bright-red **hips** that ripen in early winter. These hips have a high vitamin C content and are harvested commercially for processing into rose hip syrups. Sweet briar was originally grown as an ornamental rose and the first plants in New Zealand were grown from seed carried by early settlers. Although very beautiful, it is now a major scrub weed in the South Island. It is also found along North Island roadsides and in home gardens. This plant is also known as eglantine. The closely related dog rose, *Rosa canina,* can be found growing wild as well and is distinguished by its flower, which is white rather than pink.

Scarlet sage *Salvia coccinea*

Family Labiatae. Generally believed to be a native of Brazil, scarlet sage is a sub-shrub perennial in warmer climates and an annual in cooler climates. The plant is upright and bushy and will reach up to 90 cm high and 50–60 cm wide. Stems are square and branched with a few bristly hairs. **Leaves** are ovate, opposite, 3–5 cm long, softly hairy on both surfaces and on short stems. The showy, tubular-shaped **flowers** are bright red, about 2–3 cm long and arranged in loose whorls of three to six flowers along the upright stems. Blooms appear continuously from early summer to first frost. Plants can be found mostly in warmer and coastal areas in home gardens, parks, reserves and meadow gardens. The plant is quite tolerant of sea spray. Don't confuse this species with the popular bedding plant *Salvia splendens* (also called scarlet sage), which is a lower-growing annual with larger flowers and does not re-seed itself. *Coccinea* means 'scarlet' or 'bright, deep pink'.

Catchfly *Silene armeria*

Family Caryophyllaceae. An upright annual plant, native to Europe, growing 30–45 cm high and 20–30 cm wide. Stems and **leaves** are smooth, grey-green in colour, and the stems are sometimes sticky below the leaves. Leaves are ovate to lanceolate with smooth outer margins, 3–6 cm long and sessile to the stem. Hot pink to cerise-coloured **flowers** are arranged in umbels near the apex of the plant. Each flower is 1–2 cm across with an elongated flower capsule. Flowering is in spring and summer and plants can be found naturalising in home gardens where they can form large colonies, sometimes escaping out into waste areas. The sticky fluid that is excreted from the plant can entangle small flies, hence the

common name catchfly. The plant is also commonly called none-so-pretty. The name *Silene* probably comes from Greek *sialon*, 'saliva', referring to the gummy excretion on the stems, and/or named for *Silenus*, the intoxicated foster-father of Bacchus (god of wine) who was covered with foam, much like the glandular secretions of many species of this genus.

Breath of heaven *Silene coeli-rosa*

Family Caryophyllaceae. A native of south-west Europe and the Mediterranean. This is a very free-flowering, slender and upright annual, growing 45–60 cm high and 30–45 cm wide. Small, grey-green **leaves** are linear to lanceolate and give an overall wispy appearance to the plant. Single **flowers**, 2–4 cm across, are pink, mauve or white with a notch on the edge of each of the five petals. The eye of each flower usually is in a contrasting colour. Flowers are borne on numerous smooth, upright stems. Flowering is in summer and plants can be found naturalising in sunny areas, mostly in home gardens throughout the country. This plant has many common and botanical names. It is sometimes known as rose of heaven, rose silene or viscaria. The botanical name is synonymous with *Viscaria oculata* and *Agrostemma coeli-rosa*. *Coeli-rosa* means 'rose of the heavens'.

Hedge woundwort *Stachys sylvatica*

Family Lamiaceae. Native to Eurasia, this is a perennial herb growing up to 1 m high and spreading with a green creeping rhizome. The stems are upright in habit, square and hairy. The 4–9 cm-long **leaves** are ovate, toothed, stalked, opposite and sparsely hairy. Leaves just below the flower whorls are shorter and narrower than the other stem leaves. **Flowers** are in whorls of about 6–10 in a terminal spike. Each flower is around 15 mm across, claret-

coloured with whitish markings, the upper lip hood-shaped and lower lip divided into three obvious lobes, the middle one much the largest. The flower calyx has five sepals in which four **nutlets** develop after flowering. This plant will flower from spring to autumn and can be found frequenting shady woodland areas, country gardens, hedge banks and waste ground. If crushed the plant gives off a foul smell. The common name refers to the ancient use of this plant in staunching bleeding wounds. The name *Stachys* is from the Greek 'stachus', ear of grain or a spike, in reference to the spike-like form of the flowers.

Thyme *Thymus vulgaris*

Peter Johnson

Family Lamiaceae. Thyme is an aromatic, shrubby perennial native to the western Mediterranean region to southern Italy. It grows 20–40 cm high and up to twice as wide and forms a bushy, multi-branched, spreading mound. The stems are square and the

Peter Johnson

leaves are arranged in pairs opposite each other. The leaves are small, about 1–2 cm long, grey-green in colour, linear to oval and slightly fuzzy. Tiny lilac to purple, occasionally white, **flowers** are arranged in dense clusters near the tips of the stems. Each flower is tubular in shape, up to 1 cm long and has four lobes of almost equal size. Flowering is in spring to summer. Thyme has become well-established over several thousand hectares of dry, sunny country in Central Otago. Gold miners probably introduced it in the 1860s and 70s. This plant is also commonly found in home gardens and herb gardens. It is used in seasonings and formerly as a medicine. It is also commonly called wild thyme, common thyme and garden thyme.

Golden Spaniard *Aciphylla aurea*

Family Apiaceae. This is an evergreen perennial plant native to New Zealand. It is among the most distinctive of our native herbaceous plants. Plants form dense clumps, 90–100 cm wide, of stiff, bayonet-like, grey-green **leaves** up to 70 cm long. The leaves have yellow margins and midribs and can give a painful stab. In summer the plants bear numerous golden yellow **flowers** surrounded by long, spiny bracts on candelabra-like spikes up to 1 m tall. Plants of *Aciphylla* have either male or female flowers on separate plants. Stems on the male plant collapse when they have shed their pollen. The female stems stay upright to mature their seeds. Early European botanists were puzzled as to the need for spines on these plants as until around 200 years ago New Zealand had no herbivorous mammals. It is now believed the spines may have evolved as a protection against browsing moa. Plants can be found in the subalpine and mountain grasslands mainly in the east of the South Island. They are also planted for sand dune restoration and slope stabilisation. The Maori name is taramea and the plant is also commonly called golden speargrass.

Lady's mantle *Alchemilla mollis*

Alchemilla mollis grown in shade.

Alchemilla mollis grown in sun.

Family Rosaceae. A perennial plant native to Europe and growing 30–60 cm in height. Mounded, sprawling clumps of handsome foliage have stems at first green or blue-green turning to reddish or brownish later. Grey-green **leaves** are hairy on both sides, palmate and up to 15 cm across. They have shallow, rounded lobes with serrated edges. Plants are grown mainly for the beauty of their leaves that collect sparkling water droplets. The star-shaped **flowers** appear in intricately laced and branched heads. Each flower is around 5 mm wide and has yellow-green calyces instead of petals. Flowering is from late spring to early summer. Plants can be found naturalising throughout the country mostly in home gardens, parks and reserves. If grown in the shade plants remain green and fresh-looking all summer. Traditionally Lady's mantle has been used for curing women's ailments. Medieval alchemists collected the dew from the plant at dawn for use in their experiments to manufacture gold from common metals. Its common name refers to the Virgin Mary.

62

Peruvian lily *Alstroemeria aurea*

Family Alstromeriaceae. The Peruvian lily is a bushy, clump-forming, herbaceous perennial with tuberous roots, native to South America. The plant will grow 60–90 cm high with a spread of 60 cm. Narrow and twisted **leaves** are alternately spaced on slender upright stems. They are lanceolate in shape and grow to 10 cm long. Terminal clusters of five or six lily-like, 4–5 cm-wide **flowers** swirl around the top of stems. The flowers are yellow or orange, often with spotting and streaking, and bloom in summer. The Peruvian lily can be found naturalising in many private gardens, parks and reserves, especially in moist areas. This species can become invasive. Hybrid strains have become extremely popular commercial cut flowers and are available in a wide range of colours, including orange, yellow, red, pink, purple, lavender, salmon and

white. This is one of the 10 most popular flowers bought at Dutch auctions and it is named for Baron Claus von Alstroemer, an 18th century Swedish naturalist. The plant is synonymous with *Alstroemeria aurantiaca*.

63

Scarlet pimpernel *Anagallis arvensis*

Family Primulaceae. A low-growing European annual also commonly known as poor man's weather glass. The plant has a prostrate habit, with 15 cm-long elongated branches having square stems. If untouched the plant can form mats, since it sometimes roots at the nodes. The **leaves** are ovate, without stalks, many-ribbed and with small dark purple spots on the underside. The 1 cm-wide, saucer-shaped **flowers** have reddish-orange petals with five upright purple stamens topped with yellow anthers. Flowers open in the morning and close mid-afternoon; in damp weather they do not open at all, hence the weather reference in its alternative common name. This is a familiar weed that flowers nearly all year along roadsides, pastures, waste ground and gardens. Although it was used earlier in folk medicine it is now regarded unsafe, as touching the leaves can cause a skin rash. *Anagallis* is from two Greek words, 'ana', again, and 'agallein', to delight in, since the flowers open each time the sun strikes them and we can enjoy them anew each day.

Cape weed *Arctotheca calendula*

Family Asteraceae. A low-growing annual (sometimes perennial) plant from the Cape of Good Hope region in South Africa. This hairy plant spreads by means of runners, has a basal rosette of pinnately cut **leaves** and will grow up to 25 cm high. The tip segment of each leaf is larger than the base segments. The **flower** heads are set on single stalks and have four or five rows of greenish bracts. Pale yellow rays are tinged with green or purple underneath and surround a central mass of stamens. Cape weed flowers from spring to autumn and can be found on roadsides, waste areas and beaches and is often a common weed in lawns in the North Island. This is a smaller and paler relative of gazanias and arctotis, both of which are larger and brighter coloured. The name *calendula* comes from the Latin 'calendae', calendar, alluding to this plant's long flowering season.

Maori onion *Bulbinella hookeri*

Family Asphodelaceae. This is a tufted, deciduous, bulbous perennial native to alpine areas in both the North and South Islands of New Zealand. Clumps grow 30–60 cm high and wide and have narrow, strap-shaped, mid-green **leaves** around 50 cm

long. The roots are fleshy and edible. The flower stalk, 25–35 cm high, bears spikes of bright yellow **flowers** on the upper third of the stalk with the lower flowers opening first. Each individual flower is 6–8 mm across. Flowering is from spring to early summer. It prefers to grow in damp sites and if suited can form extensive colonies. It is most widespread and abundant in the subalpine areas and pastures of the South Island. It is resistant to burning and is unpalatable to animals. *Hookeri* is named for Sir William Jackson Hooker, author, professor of botany and director of the Royal Botanical Gardens at Kew in the mid-19th century. He participated in the Antarctic expedition of the HMS *Erebus* (1839–43) and his six-volume flora of the Antarctic islands, New Zealand and Tasmania was based on the specimens collected during this expedition.

English marigold *Calendula officinalis*

Family Asteraceae. Also commonly known as pot marigold, this is a native of the Mediterranean. Calendula is an annual with angular branched stems and prominent pale green obovate or oblanceolate **leaves** with widely spaced teeth. The whole plant stands 30–60 cm high with a bushy habit. The bright orange or yellow **flowers**, 5–6 cm across, are borne on a crown-shaped receptacle and, as the petals drop off, a circular corona of **seeds**

remains. The flowers can be either single or double. Plants are grown throughout New Zealand, mostly in private gardens. Calendula is so named because it can be found in flower through all calendar months of the year. Many cultivated varieties of marigold come from completely different genera and these should be distinguished from *Calendula officinalis*. Calendula is widely used in homeopathic remedies with tinctures and oils made from the flowers being soothing to skin irritations. It is used in many cosmetics and has edible flowers. In the 12th century some thought that merely looking at the plant would improve the eyesight, clear the head and encourage cheerfulness. Traditionally the flowers were used to impart a yellow colour to cheese.

Family Aizoaceae. A spreading, evergreen succulent plant native to coastal areas of South Africa. It has a prostrate habit, growing 10–15 cm high with woody stems that root at the nodes and grow up to 6 m long. The stems and **leaves** are very thick and fleshy. The large, lanceolate leaves, 4–6 cm long, are green, often tinged red and straight to slightly curved. They are sharply three-angled and occur in pairs, slightly united at the base. **Flowers** are 8–10 cm wide with two of the calyx lobes longer than the petals. They are pale yellow and turn pink as they age, with plants often showing both colours. Flowering continues all summer followed by **fruit** that tapers at the base into the stalk. The pulpy fruits are edible. This is an aggressive plant that can form impenetrable mats that crowd out other species, and plants can be found in coastal areas, cliffs and sand dunes throughout the country. It is often planted to assist soil or sand dune stabilisation. The leaves have medicinal properties. This plant is synonymous with *Mesembryanthemum edule* and is also commonly called Hottentot fig or pig face, referring to the fleshy leaves curling around the ripening fruit forming a snout, ears and tusks.

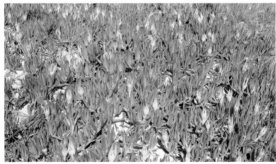

Carpobrotus edulis showing fruits.

Corn marigold *Chrysanthemum segetum*

Family Asteracae. This is an attractive upright, annual plant from the Mediterranean and North Africa. It has fleshy pinnate **leaves** that are divided almost to the midrib and are a blue-grey in colour. The plant supports stems up to 60 cm high upon which vibrant yellow **flowers**, 4–5 cm wide, sit. The rays surround a large, central, deep yellow disc. This is a very common plant that flowers nearly all year around and easily finds it way into gardens and waste areas alike, even seeding into crevices and cracks in pavements. As this is a plant that enjoys both sandy

and acidic soils you will meet it on the beach or in the old cemetery but unlike other inhabitants of the latter location this plant is here to stay. It was once a common weed of the cornfields, hence its name.

Tickseed *Coreopsis lanceolata*

Family Compositae. Tickseed is native to Central America. It is a herbaceous, branching, erect perennial with most of the leaves concentrated at the base, giving it a clumped appearance. This is a very tough plant that will increase rapidly with more and more bloom. Multiple stems rise 60–90 cm from the base. Shiny green **leaves** are opposite, linear, oblong to oblanceolate and can reach 15 cm in length. Most leaves are on the lower part of the stem and

some lower leaves may be divided. Golden-yellow, daisy-style **flowers** are up to 6 cm wide. The tips of the rays have three to five shallow lobes. Blooms first appear in late spring and continue into mid-summer. This is an attractive ground-cover for harsh sunny conditions like road-sides, pond banks, fields or sandy open ground. Almost any soil will do. **Seeds** are a favourite food for finches. Named 'tick-seed' as the seed looks like a tick (insect). Also, it is said early American settlers placed this plant in their mattresses to repel fleas and bed bugs. This is the grandfather species of many *Coreopsis* hybrids.

Plains coreopsis *Coreopsis tinctoria*

Family Compositae. From a genus of about 80 species this annual is a native of North America and is often described as the most popular of the genus. The plant will form a clump about 30 cm wide from which erect, branched stems grow around 90 cm high, sometimes higher. **Leaves** are opposite, once or twice pinnately divided into narrow linear segments. They are mid to dark green and about 10 cm long. A profusion of 4 cm-wide **flowers** with seven or eight rays sit on top of the stems. Flowers are bright yellow and red at the base. Disc florets are dark red. Flowering is from late spring to late summer. This species is widely used out of the cultivated garden, particularly on roadside verges and driveways. It is a versatile plant that will thrive in either damp or dry soils. There are two other plains coreopsis commonly found: a smaller form, growing 40–60 cm, and a dark red dwarf form that has deep mahogany red flowers. The genus *Coreopsis* is Florida's State Wildflower.

Yellow corydalis *Corydalis lutea*

Family Fumariaceae. A tuberous herbaceous plant native to Europe and Great Britain. The plant will grow 20 cm high and form a mound 30 cm wide. It can be evergreen in warm climates. Ferny, glaucous **leaves** are two or three-pinnate with distinctive three-lobed leaflets and resemble those of bleeding heart (*Dicentra*) to which it is related. Racemes of golden-yellow **flowers** surround the dissected foliage. Each tubular-shaped flower is 2–3 cm long and has four petals and short spurs. Flowers occur from spring through to late summer. Corydalis can be found throughout the country where it forms a groundcover in sunny or shaded areas. It will seed freely into pockets in old walls, cracks in the pavement or rocky outcrops and is considered a classic cottage garden plant. It is sometimes also known as yellow fumitory. The genus is named for the Greek 'korydalis', crested lark, referring to the flower shape's resemblance to the lark's head. A white form with yellow tips is also commonly found.

Yellow cosmos *Cosmos sulphureus*

Family Compositae/Asteraceae. Yellow cosmos is found native in Mexico and is a frost tender annual growing 60–90 cm high with a spread of 45 cm or more. It has rich green, feathery foliage that is coarser than that of the common cosmos, *Cosmos bipinnatus*. The **leaves** are 5–30 cm long, opposite and one or two-pinnate. Solitary, bowl-shaped **flowers** 5–7 cm across are borne on long, slender stems above the foliage. Flowers can be single or semi-double with the colour ranging from deep yellow to orange and sometimes reaching a dark, burnt orange. Flowering is from summer to autumn, often with successions of plants flowering, reseeding then flowering again within the same season. Plants thrive on well-drained, infertile soil and can be found naturalising in warm, dry sites, mostly in home gardens.

Brass buttons *Cotula coronopifolia*

Family Asteraceae. This is a creeping annual, sometimes perennial, plant native to the southern hemisphere including New Zealand. It is a creeping and rooting plant, forming low mats, 10–15 cm high, of fleshy, hairless, aromatic stems and leaves. The green **leaves** are alternate, lanceolate, 2–7 cm long and deeply toothed to pinnately lobed with the leaf bases sheathing the stems. Solitary, bright yellow, button-shaped **flower** heads, 8 mm across, are held on terminal stems above the foliage. Flowering is in spring and summer but **seeds** do not ripen until the following spring. Plants can be found throughout the country in wet areas near the coast where it can tolerate the saline conditions. It also grows inland by swamps and streams. Although considered a weed it is not noxious and is also grown in home gardens where it will tolerate both dampness and dryness. Other common names are bachelor's buttons (not to be confused with *Centaurea* species), yellow buttons and buttonweed.

Family Crassulaceae. This is a succulent shrub from a genus of 40 species and is native to South Africa. The plant will reach up to 1.3 m in height with a spread of 60 cm. The grey-green, fleshy, opposite and rounded **leaves** have red margins and a powdery bloom. They will reach up to 13 cm long by about half as wide. In summer clusters of orange to red, bell-shaped, pendulous **flowers** form on 60-cm stalks. Individual flowers are about 2–3 cm in length. The pig's ear is one of the most common cotyledons. The plant can be found on coastal rocks and sand dunes from Auckland to Otago. It can also be seen on steep coastal cliff faces where it colonises in rocky crevices. The name *Cotyledon* comes from the Greek 'cotule', a cavity, referring to the cup-like leaf shape and could also refer to the resemblance of the leaves to the first pair of leaves, the cotyledons, of many seedlings.

Family Iridaceae. Montbretia, although originally from tropical and southern Africa, is actually a hybrid of garden origin. The plant will grow up to 1 m high from a bulb-like, 3 cm-wide corm. New corms keep producing on short underground stolons. It quickly forms large, dense and spreading upright clumps. The sword-shaped **leaves** are mid-green and semi-evergreen. Slender, arching stems bear funnel-shaped **flowers** in nodding clusters on one-sided spikes. Each flower has six lobes, 5–6 cm long, and colours vary from yellow and orange to red. The zigzag axis of the flower stem is distinctive. Flowering is in summer. Plants are common throughout the country and can be found naturalising on banks, hedges, roadsides and rough ground. They can become very weedy in some situations, especially along waterways. The botanical name covers a wide range of species produced from crosses of *Crocosmia aurea* and *C. pottsii* and is synonymous with *Montbretia crocosmia*.

African daisy *Dimorphotheca aurantiaca*

Family Compositae. Native to South Africa, *Dimorphoteca aurantiaca*, synonymous with *D. sinuata*, is also commonly known as star of the Veldt or Cape marigold. The plant is a hardy annual or tender perennial, dwarf, compact and growing up to 30 cm high. Mid-green **leaves** that are narrowly oblong and alternate grow up to 8 cm. The **flowers** are about 4–6 cm in diameter and have a darker band of colour about the central disc from which the ray florets curve upwards. Colours are vivid, grading through white to salmon, yellow and orange on top of slender stems and will close at night or in dull weather. Flowers are produced in spring and summer, and plants can be found in private gardens, parks and meadow gardens, especially in very dry areas. *Dimorphotheca* comes from the Greek 'dimorph', two forms, and 'theke', ovary, indicating a plant with two different types of fruit. This refers to the two very distinct **seed** shapes: seed can be either a 'flake' (like an oat flake) or a 'stick' (miniature stick-shaped). *Dimorphotheca* is pronounced dy-mor-foh-THEE-kuh.

Indian strawberry *Duchesnea indica*

Family Rosaceae. Native to Asia, the Indian strawberry is a semi-evergreen trailing perennial growing to a height of 7–10 cm and multiplies rapidly by stolons to an indefinite spread. New plantlets take root at nodes along the stolons. The dark green **leaves** are alternate with each leaf divided into three toothed leaflets. The smooth yellow **flowers** are up to 2 cm wide and are surrounded by five three-lobed leafy bracts. Flowers look not unlike buttercup flowers. Blooms first appear in early spring and continue into autumn. Ornamental, strawberry-like, small, red **fruits** appear in late summer. Although the fruits look tasty, they are quite bland and dry and are certainly no substitute for real strawberries, genus *Fragaria*. Plants thrive in moist, shaded areas, forest margins, reserves and waste areas. It is most commonly found in the wetter, northern regions.

Californian poppy *Eschscholzia californica*

Family Papaveraceae. The Californian poppy is a perennial plant that grows 30–40 cm high with a slightly sprawling habit. Originally from north-western United States, it has feathery, blue-grey **leaves** that are several times divided into narrow lobes. The **flowers** have four large orange petals, 2–6 cm long, that have a conspicuous rim around the base of the capsule. They flower in spring and summer but only open in the sun and will close on cloudy days. Flowers are followed by cylindrical **seedpods**, 6–8 cm long. One of the most common wildflowers found growing all over New Zealand, it thrives in dry places, roadsides, shingle or gravel and will provide an amazing sight when seen growing en masse. This plant can often be seen on the shingle fans of rivers in the South Island where it helps stabilise the riverbanks, and farmers have been known to graze their stock on it. There are numerous beautiful cultivars of this species but many eventually revert to the original. This is the State Flower of California.

79

YELLOW/ORANGE

Wood spurge *Euphorbia amygdaloides* var. *robbiae*

Family Euphorbiaceae. A European native, this perennial spurge is one of many found naturalising in New Zealand. It has upright stems growing from creeping, underground rhizomes. It can reach around 60 cm high and form large, spreading patches.

Leathery, oblanceolate and glaucous, dark **leaves** are 3–7 cm long. They form a distinct rosette on the non-flowering stems. Kidney-shaped bracts join around the stems. The tiny yellow **flowers** have glands with two stout and converging horns. Prominent, yellowish-green bracts surround the flowers. Flowering is in spring and summer and plants can be found colonising lightly shaded woodland gardens, parks and reserves. The straight species *Euphorbia amygdaloides* grows somewhat taller and often has reddish stems. *E. polychroma*, cushion spurge, is also commonly found but in sunnier areas. It forms a small, bushy shrub, 25–30 cm high, with bright green, ovate leaves. Flower heads, 4–5 cm wide, consist of tiny, bright yellow flowers surrounded by showy, funnel-shaped bracts.

Euphorbia amygdaloides var. *robbiae*.

Euphorbia polychroma.

Fennel *Foeniculum vulgare*

Family Apiaceae. This is a hardy perennial herb from Europe that looks much like a tall version of dill. The plant has an erect, bushy habit, growing up to 2 m high. Polished stems bear blue-green pinnate **leaves** finely divided into threadlike segments. Leaves can be 30 cm long and 40 cm wide and are highly aromatic. In summer the plant produces clusters of tiny golden-yellow **flowers** with five tiny petals in slightly domed compound umbels. The rugby ball-shaped, small brown **seeds** are 4–9 mm long with lateral ribs, maturing

in late summer. Although the young plant is quite attractive with its feathery or ferny appearance, fennel can be highly invasive and readily colonises disturbed waste areas and roadsides throughout the country. The whole plant is strongly aromatic with a smell of aniseed and the leaves and seeds are used for seasonings.

YELLOW/ORANGE

Family Compositae. Native to North America, blanket flower is a slender, erect perennial growing 40–60 cm high and around 30 cm wide. **Leaves** are grey-green and lanceolate. Basal leaves are entire and toothed and upper leaves alternate, toothed and up to 15 cm long. Leaves and stems have coarse, greyish-white hairs. Showy, daisy-like **flower** heads, 7–8 cm wide, have reddish disc florets in the centre surrounded by ray florets that are red at the base and yellow at the rims. The **seed** has bristled scales. Flowering is from summer to autumn. Gaillardias thrive in hot, dry areas and can be found in meadow gardens and home gardens. The species name *aristata* is in reference to bristles on the seeds. Blanket flower is similar to members of the *Helianthus* genus and the *Chrysanthemum* genus, but is distinguished from these two by its flattened stem and red-based, yellow-tipped flowers. *Gaillardia pulchella*, Indian blanket, is an annual plant with characteristics similar to its perennial cousin.

Family Malvaceae. From a genus of around 200 tropical and sub-tropical species there are two that are native to New Zealand. *Hibiscus trionum* is an annual or short-lived perennial growing up to 60 cm high. It has an erect or sometimes spreading habit with rough, hairy stems. The **leaves** are mid-green, palmately lobed and 7–10 cm across. Large, creamy-white to lemon **flowers**, 5–7 cm across, with a dark maroon to chocolate-brown eye, are produced on terminal or auxiliary stems. An inflated, bladder-like calyx that bears the **seed capsule** follows flowering. *H. diversi-folius* has similar flowers but grows taller, up to 1–2 m high with woodier branches. Prickly bristles cover the branches, leaf stems and leaf midribs. Flowering is from late spring to the end of summer. These are two of our most colourful native plants. Both plants come from coastal areas of the North Island but it is fairly rare to find them growing naturally in the wild. However, they are used frequently in home landscaping, parks and reserves.

St John's wort *Hypericum perforatum*

Family Clusiaceae. From a genus of over 400 species this rhizomatous perennial plant is native to much of Europe, northern Africa and western Asia. It grows from 30–90 cm tall with numerous erect, woody stems that have two raised ridges. This is quite unusual as round or four-square stems are the general rule. It is only *Hypericum perforatum* that has these two raised edges, making the stem appear pressed flat. The **leaves** are opposite, oblong or elliptic and around 2.5 cm long. When held to the light the leaves reveal translucent dots that make them look perforated. The dots are not holes but a layer of colourless essential plant oils and resin.

The yellow, star-shaped **flowers** develop in clusters. They are 1–2 cm across, have five black-dotted petals and many prominent yellow stamens. When crushed, the flower petals may exude red-coloured oil. Flowering is in summer when plants can be found along roadsides, railway lines, pastures and waste areas. The oil in the leaves is very toxic to animals and so a leaf-feeding beetle has been used to control this plant. Traditionally St John's wort was gathered on St John's Day, 24 June, the birthday of John the Baptist, and hung above doorways or pictures to guard against evil spirits. It is still used in homeopathic medicine. *Hypericum* comes from the Greek for 'above an icon' and *perforatum* is Latin for 'perforated'.

Stinking iris *Iris foetidissima*

Family Iridaceae. A perennial, clump-forming, rhizomatous plant, native to Europe and North Africa and growing 45–90 cm high and around 60 cm wide. It is unusual in that the fruit and not the flowers are the primary ornamental trait. The tall, ever-green **leaves** are sword-shaped, shiny and 10–15 mm wide with numerous parallel veins. The **flowers** are borne on somewhat flattened stems, with two or three short branches. Several flowers open in succession. The enveloping spathes are green and leaf-like but much shorter. Colour can vary from a dull purple, or violet tinged with yellow, to pale yellow generally with darker veins on the three lower petals, known as falls. Flowering is in early summer. **Seedpods** split open in autumn to reveal rows of ornamental orange-red seeds that remain well into winter. This iris can be found in partly shady areas in home gardens, parks, reserves and grassy waste areas. Although a very pretty iris it does have a distinctive odour. The fetid smell of its name *foetidissima* or 'stinking' is brought out by crushing the leaves. The smell has been likened to that of beef and hence its other common name of roast beef plant.

Yellow flag iris *Iris pseudacorus*

Family Iridaceae. A native of Europe and North Africa, this iris grows from a thick, creeping rhizome that often pushes up through the soil surface. From above it rise the broad, flat, sword-shaped, stalkless **leaves**, bound several together into a sheath at the base. The lower leaves are 60–90 cm tall with the upper leaves much shorter surrounding the flower-stalks. These round flower stalks seldom rise as high as the outer leaves. On the top of the stalks are deep yellow **flowers**, two or three together, the buds being very large and pointed. The mature flowers consist of three large, drooping, yellow, petal-like sepals (the falls) with brownish mottled markings on their upper surfaces, inside which are three yellow stigmas that arch gracefully over the stamens. After fertilisation, the floral leaves fade and drop away from the top of the **capsule**, which increases in size. When ripe, the capsule opens above and allows the smooth, flattened **seeds**, when blown by the wind, to fall some distance away. This iris blooms from spring to early summer in damp or wet areas, even standing in water. It can be found in home gardens, riverbanks and lake edges. It is also known as the flower de Luce, or fleur de Lys, being the origin of the heraldic emblem of the kings of France and as such has many historical associations.

Tree lupin *Lupinus arboreus*

Family Fabaceae. This is a perennial, evergreen shrub native to the Pacific coast of the United States. It generally grows up to 2 m tall, sometimes taller, and around 1–2 m wide. This rapidly growing shrub has grey-green, coarsely toothed, palmate **leaves** with five or more leaflets, 3–10 mm wide, radiating out from centres. Erect, 15–25 cm racemes of fragrant, sulphur yellow to bright yellow, pea-like **flowers** are formed in whorls along the tall stems. Flowering usually begins in the plant's second spring and continues until mid-summer. The lupin flower is basically shaped like a pea flower, except that the upper petal is folded back and the lower petals are laterally compressed to form a keel. This plant is an aggressive self-seeder and it can be an invasive weed. It has colonised sand dunes in many areas of the country as well as sandy or gravelly riverbeds, roadsides and waste areas. The name *Lupinus* is believed to be derived from the Latin 'lupis', wolf, reflecting an erroneous belief that the deep-rooting plant robbed the soil of goodness. In fact the plant has good nitrogen-fixing capabilities.

Monkey musk *Mimulus guttatus*

Family Scrophulariaceae. This is an annual, sometimes short-lived perennial, native to western North America and Alaska. The plant has creeping roots and upright flowering stems growing up to 1 m high. **Leaves** are shiny, broad, in opposite pairs, roundly toothed and clasp the stems on the upper part of the plant. Yellow **flowers** are borne towards the tips of the stems in the leaf axils. Flowers are 2 cm wide and have four petals with red spots at the mouth. The throat of the flower is almost closed by hairy ridges. Flowering is from early to late summer and plants are commonly found in damp or wet places such as streambanks, ditches and swamps. The original musky smell of this plant seems to have disappeared today. The name *guttatus* is Latin for 'spotted', referring to the tiny red spots on the flowers. *Mimulus* may come either from the Greek 'mimo', an ape, because of a resemblance of the markings of the **seeds** to the face of a monkey, or from Latin

'mimus', an actor or mimic, because the flower is like the mouthpiece of the grinning masks worn by classical actors. *Mimulus moschatus* is also a short-lived perennial growing 50 cm high and has long, hairy and slimy stems. Flowers are similar but have thin, dark veins and no spots. *Mimulus repens* is a New Zealand native with a creeping habit found growing in salt marshes. It has large purple flowers.

Evening primrose *Oenothera glazioviana*

Family Onagraceae. The evening primroses are a group of yellow-flowered plants that range from short 'sundrops' to tall ones like this species. This upright, biennial plant is native to North America and grows 1 m plus. Basal **leaves** form a large rosette in the first year followed by tall, branched, leafy **spikes**. The leaves are mid-green, lanceolate, 8–20 cm long and gradually reduce in size up the stems. Light yellow **flowers**, 5–7 cm across, are widely funnel-shaped and have long, often reddish, buds. The flowers start to bloom in late afternoon and continue all night into early morning. The scented flowers are hermaphrodite (have both male and female organs) and are pollinated by moths, butterflies and bees. Flowering is in summer and plants can be found along dry roadsides and in waste areas, meadows and home gardens. There is some confusion as to the origin of this plant with the general thought that it could be a garden hybrid. It is synonymous with *Oenothera lamarckiana*. *O. stricta* is also commonly found along dry roadsides and waste areas. It is smaller-growing and can be distinguished by the older flowers turning reddish-orange as they fade. *O. biennis* is tall, with smaller, bright yellow flowers.

Oenothera stricta.

89

Creeping buttercup *Ranunculus repens*

Family Ranunculaceae. This plant originates from Europe, North Africa and south-west Asia, and is probably the most widespread of the buttercup species in New Zealand. The creeping

buttercup is a deep-rooted, clump-forming perennial growing up to 60 cm high with thick runners that can grow up to 1 m long, taking root at the nodes. The **leaves**, about 4 cm long by 5 cm wide, are on long stalks and divided into three deeply toothed lobes, the central lobe on a short stalk. The stem leaves are smaller with shorter stalks. The **flowers** are in clusters on long stems arising from the leaf axils, 1–2 cm across, and have five shiny yellow petals and five spreading, hairy sepals. Flowering is in spring and summer and plants can be found in abundance in poorly drained lawns, pastures, waste areas and orchards, and also in crops and gardens throughout the country. *Ranunculus acris*, giant buttercup, is also commonly found in damp pastures. It is taller, growing up to 1 m, has slightly larger flowers and leaves deeply divided into three to seven lobes. Cattle do not eat either of these pasture weeds and so they can become very invasive. *Ranunculus* comes from Latin 'rana', little frog, because many species tend to grow in moist places.

Scabweeds *Raoulia* species

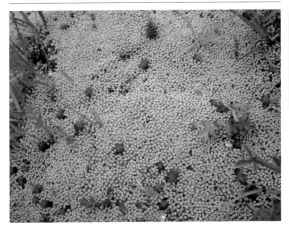

Family Asteraceae. This is rather large genus with at least 20 species belonging to New Zealand. Plants of the low-growing scabweeds, including *Raoulia haastii*, *R. australis*, *R. hookeri*, *R. tenuicaulis* and *R. grandiflora*, are found on stony riverbeds and subalpine regions. They form large, tight, flat mats and spread over dry river stones and rocks, often binding the stony ground together. Plants vary in size, growing up to 1 m wide, but seldom more than 2–3 cm high. **Leaves** are thick, usually greyish and 5 mm long by 2 mm wide and often silky or woolly. *R. haastii* has green, moss-like leaves. Tiny **flowers**, usually yellow, 3–7 mm across, are surrounded by papery bracts. *R. tenuicaulis* and *R. grandiflora* have tiny white flowers. Flowering is in summer. Other *Raoulia* species such as *R. eximia* and *R. mammillaris* are known as vegetable sheep. These extraordinary plants form huge, thick hummocks that sprawl over rocks and stones in alpine regions. From a distance these plants can resemble a sheep, hence the name. Many of the lowland species are grown in parks, reserves and home gardens.

Mignonette *Reseda luteola*

Family Resedaceae. A European native biennial plant with a leafy, upright and branching habit. The plant grows a rosette in the first year, followed by thick and sturdy stems, up to 1 m high. These stems carry alternate, narrow, lanceolate, sessile, green **leaves** up to 8 cm long. The basal leaves turn yellow and orange during the summer. Abundant spikes of tiny greenish-yellow **flowers** sit above the foliage. Each flower, 4–5 mm across, has four sepals and four divided petals. Plants can be found colonising open, stony and sandy places, often in large patches, especially in lower South Island. This plant is also known as Dyer's rocket and weld, because of the yellow dye derived from it. The use of *Reseda* as a dye plant was first recorded in the late Roman period. *Reseda lutea* is a similar plant but smaller, 30–60 cm tall with a more branching habit. *Reseda alba* is tall-growing with spikes of tiny white flowers and is commonly found in dry and stony places, parks, reserves and home gardens. Although from the same family as the common mignonette, *R. odora*, these plants do not have the strong perfume that this annual is renowned for.

Reseda alba.

Black-eyed Susan *Rudbeckia hirta*

Family Asteraceae/Compositae. A North American native biennial, the black-eyed Susan typically stays in a basal rosette in its first year and then produces upright, branching flowering stems, up to 1 m high and 60 cm wide, in its second year. Flowering can occur in the first year as well. **Leaves** are oblong to lanceolate, around 10 cm long, alternate and mostly basal with coarse hairs. Bristly flowering stems branch freely and bear hairy, lance-shaped leaves, 5–8 cm long. Solitary **flowers**, up to 8 cm wide, consist of an outer ring of 10–20 golden yellow ray florets and a central receptacle, often distinctly conical, composed of many dark brown to black disc florets. Flowering is in summer and autumn and after flowering and seed maturation, the plant will die. Rudbeckias can mostly be found in meadow and home gardens. The 'Gloriosa' form has a very large flower head, up to 15 cm across, with yellow, gold, chestnut or bronze rays. Although this plant has been altered from the original parent it is often considered a wildflower as it comes true from seed. *Hirta* means 'hairy'.

YELLOW/ORANGE

Family Crassulaceae. A perennial succulent plant from Europe, Western Asia and North Africa, growing 5–10 cm high. It has a moss-like appearance and grows in small, bumpy mats. Stems spread out by prostrate runners. **Leaves** are small, fat, succulent, ovate, 3–10 mm long and mid to yellow green in colour. Young leaves have reddish tips. **Flowers**, up to 20 mm across, are yellow

with five pointed petals in a star-like arrangement. The flowers occur at the tips of the stems. Flowering is in spring and summer and vast colonies can be found naturalising in stony and dry rocky areas in the lower South Island where they can turn the hillsides yellow. The plant is also commonly used in home gardens, especially rock gardens and dry banks. This plant is sometimes also called gold moss sedum or biting stonecrop. The species name *acre* comes from the Latin for 'sharp, pungent'. The leaves have a sharp peppery taste and are unpalatable. A cultivated form with bright golden foliage is also commonly found.

Mullein *Verbascum thapsus*

Family Scrophulari-aceae. Verbascum is a biennial plant native to Europe. The plant produces a basal rosette of large, thick, fuzzy **leaves** in the first year. These obovate to oblanceolate leaves, 8–40 cm long, are covered in downy, soft white, branched hairs, have narrowly winged stalks and often survive through the winter under the snow. In the second year, mullein sends up a stoutly erect flower stalk up to 2 m high. The upper leaves are stalkless, upward-pointing and act as funnels, col-lecting moisture and sending it down the plant. The yellow **flowers**, 2–3 cm across, appear in densely packed spikes and bloom randomly from spring until autumn. Vast quantities of seeds are produced, and these

Verbascum virgatum.

may remain dormant in the soil for many years. Mullein can become invasive by quickly colonising disturbed areas and plants can be found in dry waste areas, roadsides, riverbeds and pastures. The hairs on the leaves were traditionally made into candle-wicks, and sometimes the entire stem was used as a flare. Animals won't eat mullein because the hairs irritate their mucous membranes.

Another common name is Aaron's rod. *Verbascum virgatum*, moth mullein, is similar but smaller and has greener, nearly hairless stems and leaves. Plants colonise similar areas.

Bidibidi *Acaena* species

Family Rosaceae. About 20 species of bidibidi are native to New Zealand but opinions differ as to their distinction. All are creeping, soft-stemmed plants typically growing clustered together to form large mats where individual plants are indistinguishable. Stems are prostrate to erect depending on environmental conditions and have woody stolons that root at the nodes. Foliage colour varies with different species, from blue-grey to purple and bright green. Pinnately divided **leaves** are evenly toothed and 2–6 cm long. Round, ball-shaped, white **flower** heads, 2–3 cm across, are held 10–15 cm above the leaves and in some species are very showy. Flowering time varies from spring to mid-summer. Flower heads then turn brown and spiny as the **seed** ripens. Prominent spines often have hooked or barbed tips that easily attach themselves to clothing or animal coats, thus spreading far and wide. Plants can be found throughout New Zealand in riverbeds, grasslands, alpine and open places and some are considered noxious weeds. The common name of bidibidi (with various spellings) or biddybid is an anglicisation of the Maori name piripiri.

Yarrow *Achillea millefolium*

Family Asteraceae. Herbaceous perennial with extensive creeping rhizomes and erect, furrowed, woolly stems up to 60 cm high. It is native to Great Britain and Eurasia. The dark green **leaves** are deeply, pinnately divided, giving it an overall ferny appearance. The basal rosette of leaves may remain green right throughout the winter. Flattened **flower** heads, 10–15 cm wide, consist of a cluster of tiny, tubular discs with short, muddy white to pinkish ray flowers in a typical umbrella form. Flowering is from spring to autumn. Yarrow is often seen growing in lawns as it can survive mowing and will often bloom even at ground level. It is frequently seen along roadsides and waste ground where it occupies dry, open sites in a variety of habitats. It is an invader species that will increase rapidly. Generally it is unpalatable, although domestic livestock and wildlife occasionally consume the flowers. Although classed as a weed the young leaves are sometimes eaten in salads and the flowers used for summer and winter bouquets. When cut fresh and kept in water, yarrow flavours the air with an aromatic spiciness. Yarrow is an ancient herb steeped in mythology and is named after the Greek hero Achilles, who is said to have used the herb to heal his soldiers' wounds. During the American Civil War yarrow was widely used to treat wounds and became known as soldiers' woundwort.

Onion weed *Allium triquetrum*

Family Alliaceae. A moderately hardy bulb from Europe and Great Britain growing up to 30 cm high. At the root base a small white bulb forms clumps that can quadruple in size every year. **Leaves** are mid-green, strap-shaped and keeled. When the leaves are crushed they have a strong onion smell. The **flower** stalk is triangular in cross-section and produces 3–5 cm-wide umbels sitting above the foliage. The umbels have bell-shaped, drooping, white flowers in spring. It is an invasive pest of woodland gardens and is often seen naturalising along roadsides, waterways and waste areas. This plant is also known as wild garlic and can become an abundant and troublesome weed: the flower is pretty, but don't let it win you over. Because it spreads by both seed and bulb offsets, it can be difficult to eradicate from an area once it has been established. All parts of this plant are edible.

Family Apiaceae. *Ammi majus* is an annual, sometimes known as Queen Anne's lace, native to north-eastern Africa and Eurasia. It is a prolific grower that comes quickly into flower and blooms heavily in spring and summer. This is a tall-growing species, usually around 90 cm, but can grow up to 2 m. It has upright stems with multiple branches with three-pinnate, light-green, lance-shaped **leaves**. Compound umbels, 10–15 cm wide, comprise about 10 tiny white **flowers** per umbel, closely resembling lace work. Don't confuse this plant with the roadside Queen Anne's lace, *Daucus carota*, which is a common weed and considered a pest. *Ammi majus* is common in the cut-flower trade, adding a lacy delicate look to bouquets and lasts 3–10 days as a cut flower. Mostly it is found growing in private gardens but is also used to attract beneficial insects into horticultural crops. The ancient Egyptians used it as treatment for certain skin diseases and today it has a range of medicinal uses. Bishop's flower is also used as an aromatic spice that has a flavour of thyme.

WHITE

Family Asteraceae. Native to New Zealand, this is a prostrate or hanging perennial with woody stems, growing 20–24 cm high with spreading branches forming quite a large patch. The shiny **leaves** are sessile, alternate, dark green and 5–10 cm long with white tomentum below. The daisy-like **flowers** occur in clusters, 7–10 cm across, at the end of long stalks. This distinguishes them from the *Helichrysum* species that have single, terminal flower heads. Each flower is 15 mm across, yellow and surrounded by white, papery bracts. Flowering is in spring and summer. Cudweeds are common plants that colonise shaded roadside cuttings and can be found trailing on damp, shady banks in lowland and subalpine regions from the middle of the North Island southwards, particularly in the western South Island. *Anaphalis keriense* is also commonly found in the same areas but has a narrower leaf and is commonly called by its Maori name, puatea. They were previously included in the *Gnaphalium* genus.

Japanese anemone *Anemone japonica*

Family Ranunculaceae. This is a hardy, herbaceous, perennial plant of European origin. It has a fibrous rooting system and can form clumps 60 cm or more high with a spread of several metres wide. **Leaves** are three or five-lobed, deeply cut and mid to deep green. Each stem bears a ring of leaves about two-thirds up from the base. The crisp, white, solitary **flowers** sit on top of the stems and are 3–4 cm across with six or seven petals (sometimes more) surrounding a central mass of yellow stamens. It flowers from late summer to autumn and will thrive in open woodland environments. Sometimes known as windflower, this is a popular flower for pollen-loving bees and certain flies as it

produces large quantities of pollen. There are at least 150 species and hybrids in this genus, many of which are frequently seen naturalising in parks and private gardens.

101

WHITE

Family Liliaceae. Rengarenga is from a genus of 12 species of perennial herbs mostly native to Australia but two are endemic to New Zealand. *Arthropodium cirratum* is a lily that colonises coastal situations throughout most of the North Island and the top half of the South Island. The plant forms large clumps of broad, green, fleshy, strap-shaped **leaves** up to 80 cm long. Leaves sometimes have a glaucous overtone. Panicles of white **flowers** occur on stems up to 1 m high in early summer in great abundance. The six-petalled flowers, 2.5 cm across, have purple and yellow stamens that hang downwards and are curled at the ends. This gives the plant its name of *cirratum*, meaning curled. In autumn **seed** capsules ripen to shining jet black. Rengarenga, also known as reinga lily or rock lily, is commonly used for street and commercial landscaping as well as in home gardens. Maori used this plant as a food source and for medicinal, spiritual and other cultural purposes. *A. candidum*, star lily, the other native New Zealand species, is much smaller, grows to about 30 cm high and is grass-like in appearance.

102

Italian arum *Arum italicum*

Family Araceae. This stemless woodland species is a tuberous perennial native to Europe, growing 30–35 cm in both height and width. The arrowhead-shaped, glossy greyish-green **leaves** with pale green midribs often with various markings emerge in autumn and are evergreen in warm winter climates. However, in cold areas the leaves die in winter with new leaves emerging in early spring. In all climates, foliage goes dormant in summer.

Each **flower** consists of an erect, finger-like spadix covered with minute, creamy white flowers and surrounded by a light-green, sheath-like spathe. Flowers are produced in spring. After blooming, the leaves and spathe die back, leaving only the thick spadix, which develops attractive, bright orange-red **berries** in summer. Also known as lords and ladies, the Italian arum can be found naturalising in private gardens, parks and reserves where it will quickly spread in sunny or part-shady conditions. All parts of this plant are toxic.

Lawn daisy *Bellis perennis*

Family Asteraceae. A genus of 15 species of hardy perennials native to Europe and Asia Minor. This tufted plant grows up to a height of about 10 cm and has ovate, mid-green, 5 cm-long **leaves** that form a rosette close to the ground. Stems rise from the rosette upon which the **flowers,** 2–3 cm wide, are borne. The flowers are arranged in white rays, sometimes tinged with pink, circling a yellow disc, and will close at night or in wet weather. Flowering is from spring to late summer. This is a common lawn weed found all over New Zealand. Traditionally this daisy has been a measure of love and a tribute to lovelorn maidens who plucked petals one by one to the chant 'He loves me, he loves me not'. Since nearly all daisies have an odd number of petals the answer will always be the first phrase. The name *Bellis* comes from the Latin for 'pretty'.

Greater quaking grass *Briza maxima*

Family Gramineae. This is an annual grass found native in the Mediterranean region. It has a graceful, upright habit, growing 30–60 cm high and around 30 cm wide. Narrow, pointed, bright green **leaves** are sparse and turn brown as the season progresses. The upper part of each threadlike stem carries a loose panicle of pendant, heart-shaped or oval **spikelets** that dangle on the stems (a spikelet is the basic unit of a grass **flower**  head). They are open, puffy with overlapping scale-like **seeds**, reddish-brown or bronze touched with green. The flower heads quake or rattle in the wind when the dry and papery scales rub and scrape together, giving it the plant's common name of quaking grass. Flowering is from summer to autumn and plants can be found naturalising in open, waste areas, roadsides, dry, rocky places and home gardens. *Briza media* and *B. minor* are similar but with much smaller flower heads. They are also commonly called quaking grass or shivery grass. *Briza* comes from the Greek 'britho', balance, referring to the delicately suspended spikelets.

105

WHITE

Family Asteraceae. New Zealand has nearly 60 species of *Celmisia* and this is one of the largest. It is a large, robust, perennial plant reaching 60–75 cm high, often with several tufted plants in a clump. **Leaves** are large and leathery, 20–50 cm long, silvery-grey with dense white tomentum below. Their margins are smooth and slightly recurved. The flower stems, up to 10 or more per tuft, reach around 40 cm and have several narrow leafy bracts all covered in white tomentum. The large **flower** head, 4–10 cm across, has fine white rays surrounding a large, yellow central disc. Flowering is in summer. The plant is widely distributed throughout the South Island mountains in alpine scrub and tussock regions. *Celmisia specatablis*, cotton daisy, is smaller, growing 20–50 cm high and often forming large patches. The upper leaf surface is green, smooth and shiny and the bottom clothed in white tomentum. The daisy flowers are similar to the above and plants can be commonly found in subalpine and alpine grasslands in both the North and South Islands. Plants of many *Celmisia* species are grown in parks, reserves and home gardens.

Oxeye daisy *Chrysanthemum leucanthemum*

Family Asteraceae. Closely related to *Chrysanthemum maximum*, this species is smaller but more widely spread. This is a slightly hairy European perennial that forms slender, ever-green clumps up to 60 cm high. The dark green **leaves** with irregularly toothed margins clasp the lower part of the stems. Large, solitary **flower** heads are of a classic daisy form with white petals surrounding a yellow eye. Flower size varies from around 4–8 cm across. The oxeye daisy is a common weed found in grassy fields and roadside verges where it will often crowd out other plants. It flowers from spring to autumn. Sheep, goats and horses will eat this plant, but cows and pigs do not like it. When cattle pastures are managed with a low stock density and a continuous grazing regime the plant will spread rapidly. Under these conditions, cows repeatedly select their preferred plants and will ignore this unpalatable species. A vigorous daisy can produce 26,000 seeds per plant. This plant is also known as *Leucanthemum vulgare*.

Shasta daisy *Chrysanthemum maximum*

Family Asteraceae. A perennial daisy from the Pyrenees that forms dense, evergreen, expanding clumps. Shasta daisy is a coarse species growing up to 90 cm tall with dark green **leaves**

that are lanceolate and toothed. Large, single, white **flowers**, 10 cm across with a golden eye, are borne on strong, single stems in summer and early autumn. The flowers are excellent for cutting, lasting up to 10 days in a vase. Plants will easily colonise open woodland areas and are not mindful of sun or shade. The shasta daisy is a traditional garden plant that can be found in many private gardens, parks and reserves. This is a plant with as many as 48 named cultivars ranging from white to yellow flowers, often in dwarf or double forms. This daisy is somewhat larger, taller but less aggressive than the common wild oxeye daisy, *Chrysanthemum leucanthemum*.

Wild carrot *Daucus carota*

Family Apiaceae. Somewhat variable in its growth, this European native, biennial plant is also commonly known as Queen Anne's lace. The tough erect stems reach up to 1 m high and all parts are very bristly and with a distinctive carrot odour. It bears large, three-pinnate, feathery **leaves**. The white **flowers** are grouped in slightly convex umbels, often with reddish flowers in the centre of each umbel. Each umbel changes as the flower ages, beginning with a rolling inwards form which protects the young buds, opening to a wide disc; then as the seeds ripen the form again closes inwards like a claw. The **seeds** are covered with numerous little bristles arranged in five rows. Wild carrot is an invasive weed found growing in waste areas and roadsides all over New Zealand. It flowers from spring to autumn. This wild form of the cultivated carrot is edible when young but the yellowish, spindle-shaped root (especially the centre) soon gets tough. It is similar to but much less attractive than the other known Queen Anne's lace, *Ammi majus*.

Blueberry *Dianella nigra*

Family Phormiaceae. Although this comes from a genus of around 25 species in Australasia, this is the only one endemic to New Zealand. It is a perennial, clump-forming plant growing to

about 60–80 cm high. Tufts of narrow, green, shiny, strap-like **leaves** grow 30–60 cm, sometimes 1 m, long. Panicles of insignificant flowers grow on wiry stalks 25–40 cm long. The **flower** is white, around 10 mm wide, with prominent yellow stamens. Flowering is in spring followed by small, round or oblong **berries,** greenish-brown in colour and maturing to a bright purplish-blue. Plants can be found on both moist and dry, shady banks, woods and scrubland throughout the country. It is commonly grown in parks, reserves and home gardens and is also known by its Maori name turutu. The plant is synonymous with *Dianella intermedia*. The name *Dianella* comes from the Latin 'Diana', goddess of the woods.

Mexican daisy *Erigeron karvinskianus*

Family Asteraceae. Mexican daisy is a vigorous evergreen, perennial groundcover up to 30 cm tall and native to Mexico. It has rigid, much-branched stems that spread out to lie flat along the ground, occasionally with upright growth, and will sprawl to around 70 cm. Plants will take root at the nodes, thereby developing thick mats. The upper **leaves** are small, narrow and elliptical and the lower leaves usually have three lobes. Leaves are pleasant-smelling when crushed. The prolific **flowers** are approximately 2 cm in diameter, usually white flushed with pink with yellow central discs. They can be solitary or in clusters and produce masses of fluffy **seeds**. In northern areas it will flower all year round, and in southern areas from spring to autumn. The Mexican daisy has naturalised widely and can be found colonising rock walls, stony places, waste areas and roadsides. It has been classified as a weed. *Erigeron* is Greek meaning 'early old man', referring to the fluffy, white seed heads.

Wild strawberry *Fragaria vesca*

Family Rosaceae. Wild strawberry is native to Europe and temperate regions of Asia. It is a perennial plant with a prostrate, creeping habit, growing 10–15 cm high. Plants take root at the nodes where new plantlets form. Coarsely serrated, trefoil-shaped **leaves**, up to 8 cm across, are bright green with silky hairs on top. **Flowers** are 1–2 cm wide, with white petals surrounding a raised, yellow conical centre and produced in large sprays. The centremost terminal flower opens first, is the largest and produces the largest fruit. Flowering is in spring to early summer followed by bright red, edible fruit developing below the leaves. The fruit is much smaller than commercial strawberries and it was this plant that was crossed with a South American species to give us our garden strawberry. Plants can be found in damp waste areas, along roadsides, open fields, forest margins and parks and reserves. Both the leaves and the fruit have medicinal properties. Plants are also commonly called alpine strawberries. *Fragaria* comes from the Latin 'fraga', fragrant, referring to the fragrance of the fruit.

Baby's breath *Gypsophila elegans*

Family Caryophyllaceae. A light and airy annual native to Ukraine, Caucasus, Turkey and Iran. The plant has a much-branched, upright habit, growing to 40–45 cm high and 20–30 cm wide. Delicate stems bear hairless, light-green, narrow, oblong to linear **leaves**, 1–6 cm long and 3 mm wide. Open, airy clusters of small, white, sometimes veined **flowers** with five rounded petals are 10–12 mm wide and are formed in branched panicles. These tiny flowers are prized for the lovely effect they produce in floral arrangements. The plant has a short blooming season usually in spring to early summer, performing best in cool to warm weather. It is found principally in home gardens in most areas of the country. *Gypsophila* is from the Greek 'gypos', gypsum, and 'philos', loving, as some species like growing on lime; *elegans* means elegant. The perennial *Gypsophila paniculata* has smaller, double flowers and is more sought after by florists, although this annual form also makes an excellent cut flower.

Everlasting daisy *Helichrysum belliodides*

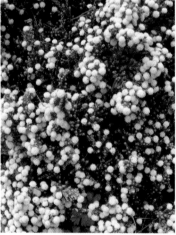

Helichrysum intermedium.

Family Asteraceae. A native New Zealand plant and probably the most common species found. It is a low-growing sub-shrub with trailing or creeping and rooting stems up to 50 cm long, and sometimes forming quite large patches. The oblong **leaves** are closely placed along the stems, usually grey-green with white tomentum below and about 5–6 mm long. **Flowers** are produced singly on short stalks from the tips of woolly stems. Each flower is 2–3 cm across with yellow centres surrounded by white, papery, petal-like bracts. Flowering is from late spring to summer. This plant is widespread in the lowland to subalpine regions of the central North Island southwards in rocky places, open grassland, scrub and roadside banks. *Helichrysum intermedium* or common helichrysum is quite different, being a well-branched, 60 cm-high shrub with crowded branches enclosed by thick, triangular scale leaves. These scaly leaves are dark green and are outlined with white hairs. The branches are tipped with yellow to white sessile flower heads that are wider than the leaf stems they terminate. It grows in rocky lowland to alpine areas in the South Island.

114

Maori calceolaria *Jovellana sinclairii*

Family Scrophulariaceae. This plant is a native New Zealand species found in the North Island from East Cape to Hawke's Bay. It is a soft, sub-shrubby plant growing up to 30 cm high and wide. The light green, ovate **leaves** are soft with serrated edges and up to 8 cm long. **Flowers** are abundantly produced in branched

panicles held up on long stems above the foliage. The pouch-shaped flowers, 1–2 cm wide, are white with purple spots inside and face downwards. Flowers are produced over a long period in spring and summer. The plants are tender and can be found in damp places along stream-sides, forest margins and sheltered, shady, moist areas. This is a threatened plant in its natural environ-ment but is common-ly found growing in home gardens, parks and reserves. This plant is closely relat-ed to *Calceolaria*, differing in that the two lobes or pockets of its flower are more equal in size, compared with the one big and one tiny lobes of *Calceolaria*.

WHITE

Family Iridaceae. A small genus with four of the species native to New Zealand. *Libertia grandiflora* is a large, perennial, tufted plant forming clumps around 50 cm high and wide. The long and narrow, strap-like, green **leaves** are up to 60 cm long and droop gracefully. Flower **spikes** have panicles of 3 cm-wide, pure white **flowers,** each with three small sepals behind three larger petals. Flowering is in spring and summer and plants can be found in lowland or damp areas and hillside forest margins in the North Island and upper South Island. *L. ixioides* is very similar but a smaller plant with the flower spikes set among, rather than above, the foliage. Plants are commonly found naturalising in lowland bush and scrub and roadsides. *L. peregrinans* has a creeping habit growing to about 40 cm with erect, green leaves with a brownish-orange midrib. The flowers are also set among the foliage. It is found in damp, sandy soils. Libertias are often called New Zealand iris and are frequently grown in parks, reserves and home gardens.

Libertia peregrinans.

Sweet alyssum *Lobularia maritima*

Family Cruciferae/Brassicaceae. Native to the Mediterranean area, this is an annual growing 15 cm tall. It has a woody base with many branched stems spreading 30 cm wide. Narrow, linear, silvery-haired **leaves**, about 1 cm long, are densely scattered along

the stems. Domed flower heads are made up of clusters of tiny, 6 mm-wide blooms. The **flowers** are usually white but sometimes are slightly rose-coloured. The flower heads elongate as they mature and have a strong, sweet-smelling fragrance. Flowering is very dense, giving an overall mound of solid colour. Flowering is nearly all year around with small, round, hairy **seedpods** being produced continually. This is a very strong self-seeder with plants finding their way into cracks and crevices, paths, driveways and rocky or sandy seaside places. Plants have been commonly and historically used as garden border edging plants. *Lobularia* is derived from the Latin for 'a small pod', referring to the fruit, and *maritima*, meaning 'of the sea'.

Swamp musk *Mazus radicans*

Family Scrophulariaceae. This is a dense, flat, carpet-forming perennial plant native to New Zealand. The slender stems take root as they creep along. The plant has unusual bronze-green **leaves** with stippled brown markings. Leaves are hairy, 2–3 cm long, obovate and closely attached to the stem. In summer the plant sends up almost stemless, two-lipped, pea-like, fragrant

flowers. Each flower is 1.5 to 2 cm across with the upper lip violet and bi-lobed and the lower lip white and tri-lobed. The flower throat has a band of yellow hairs. The flowers will close rapidly if touched. Plants can be found growing naturally along edges of bogs in subalpine regions of the country. *Mazus pumilio* is a similar plant found in lowland, swampy areas. The leaves are longer, less hairy and the flowers less showy. Both plants are cultivated and can be found in home gardens, parks and reserves in moist, well-drained sun to lightly shaded areas. *Mazus* is named from the Greek signifying a breast, erroneously given in allusion to the supposed swollen corolla or fused flower petals.

Trailing African daisy *Osteospermum fruticosum*

Family Asteraceae. This is a sprawling, evergreen perennial plant growing around 30 cm high, native to South Africa. The plant will grow from one root and spreads by smooth, woody, reddish stems that do not take root as they grow. **Leaves** are oblanceolate, mid-green, fleshy and around 6 cm long. Flower stalks support solitary **flower** heads and are lightly hairy. Flowers are traditional daisy-style, 5 cm across with a small central disc of tiny, dark blue flowers. Petal rays are usually white on the upper side and bluish mauve on the underside. Pink or mauve petals are also common. Flowers close in the evening or on cloudy days and flowering is in spring and summer. The whole plant has a light, musty smell. This plant can be found in coastal or temperate areas, banks, cliffs and home gardens. There are also a number of cultivated forms found. This daisy is also sometimes called dimorphotheca. The name *fruticosum* is from Latin 'frutex', a shrub, therefore, shrubby or bushy.

Mountain pinatoro *Pimelia oreophila*

WHITE

Family Thymelaeaceae. The genus *Pimelia* is almost exclusively Australasian with many species being very difficult to discriminate between. Mountain pinatoro is probably the most commonly found New Zealand species. It is a prostrate, mat-forming shrub

growing around 10–15 cm high and 30–40 cm wide. It has brownish stems with older branches that are scarred with rings left by falling leaves. The **leaves** are 4–8 mm long with the upper surface greyish-green and silky, haired margins that are often reddish when young. The white, sweetly scented **flowers**, about 6 mm across, are in clusters at the tips of the branches. Flowering is in summer followed by fleshy, oval-shaped, inconspicuous **berries**. Plants can be found naturally in the lowland and subalpine mountain regions of both the North and South Islands. This is also a useful landscaping plant for parks, reserves and home gardens. *Pimelia prostrata*, New Zealand daphne, is a sweetly scented, prostrate shrub also found throughout the country and has a lower-growing and sprawling habit.

Creeping pratia *Pratia angulata*

Family Lobeliaceae. From a genus of about 20 species, creeping pratia is one of four that are native to New Zealand. It is a low-growing, creeping and rooting plant that often forms large mats up to 1.5 m wide. The **leaves**, on short stalks, are ovate to oblong, vary from 4–12 mm long and have a few coarse teeth around the margins. **Flowers** are white with purple streaks and vary from 7 to 20 mm long. They are very freely produced from spring to autumn on slender stalks. These stalks elongate as shining purplish-red **berries** ripen from summer to autumn. Plants can be commonly found throughout the country in lowland to low alpine regions in damp grasslands, banks or streamsides. Plants are also commonly grown in parks, reserves and home gardens. The Maori name is panakenake. *Pratia macrodon*, mountain pratia, is a similar plant and is commonly found in mountain areas of the South Island. It is distinguished by having more deeply toothed, thicker leaves and pointed flower petals. *P. physaloides* is also similar but has blue flowers.

121

WHITE

Family Primulaceae. A small, creeping perennial plant from a genus of about 100 species but this is the only one native to New Zealand. It is a sprawling, well-branched plant growing around 5–10 cm high but spreading widely. The mid-green **leaves** are spathulate and often recurved. They are thick, shiny, 1–3 cm long and alternately placed along the stems. The white **flowers** are upward-facing, sitting on short stems above the foliage, either at the stem tips or from the leaf axils. The primrose-like flowers are around 6–10 mm across with five petals and are produced in profusion from spring to summer. Plants can be found in coastal sea marshes and rocky areas near the sea throughout the country. This plant is also native to Australia where it is called creeping brookweed. *Samolus* is a Latin name referring possibly to this plant's curative power.

Arum lily *Zantedeschia aethiopica*

Family Araceae. A robust, marsh-loving, deciduous perennial native to South Africa. The plant has a thick rhizome, will grow 60–90 cm high and form a tuft of succulent stalks with lush, green, arrow-shaped **leaves**. The leaf size will vary according to the amount of shade. A stout basal stalk, 1–1.5 m high, bears a large, funnel-shaped **flower** with a rolling, flaring waxy-white spathe, 20–25 cm long, surrounding a bright yellow spadix.

Flowering is from spring to autumn, although there may be flowering during the winter months in warm areas. It is an excellent cut flower. The white arum forms large colonies in marshy areas and can be found throughout the country. Although called the arum lily, it is neither an arum (genus *Arum*) nor a lily (genus *Lilium*), but it is associated with the lily as a symbol of purity. The leaves of the arum are very interesting in that they contain water stomata. This means they can discharge excess water by a process known as 'guttation', which prevents waterlogging and enables the arum lily to grow in wet conditions.

MIXED

Family Asteraceae. A fast-growing perennial species native to Africa. The plant will grow 30–40 cm high with a prostrate spreading or trailing habit. **Leaves** and stems are woolly, giving a silvery-green appearance. The narrow leaves are toothed and grow around 10 cm long. Solitary **flower** heads are large and showy and up to 10 cm wide. Central discs are usually dark brown or black and surrounded by rays of petals in a wide colour range from yellow to orange, apricot, cream, purple and bronze. Flowers often have a contrasting colour at the base, forming a ring around the central disc. Flowering is from spring to late summer, often longer. Plants can be found in home gardens, roadsides, wastelands, banks, riversides and sand dunes in warmer temperate areas of the country. Arctotis is often used for coastal sand dune stabilisation. Flowers close at night and may only partially open up on cloudy days. This plant is also commonly called African daisy but should not be confused with the *Dimorphotheca* species, also called African daisies.

Canna lily *Canna indica*

Family Cannaceae. The canna can look like a banana tree without the trunk and is in fact related to the banana and ginger families. It is from the West Indies and South America. This perennial plant has wide, furled **leaves** growing from a thick, multiple-eyed rhizome, just like their larger, edible cousins, and will grow 100–180 cm high. The leaves are oval, can be green or bronze-purple and grow up to 60 cm long. Yellow or red

flowers are tubular and flared, 6–8 cm long. Each flower has three petals, three sepals and three highly modified showy petal-like stamens. Flowers are followed by capsules with round, shot-like **seeds**. Seeds have been used as shot, hence another common name, Indian shot. Cannas can be found in more temperate parts of the country, along roadsides, waste ground, driveways, private gardens, parks and reserves. Many are hybrids so the size, colour and shape can vary considerably. *Canna* is from the Greek for a type of reed.

Garland daisy *Chrysanthemum coronarium*

Family Asteraceae. Originating from the Mediterranean, the garland daisy is an upright, annual plant growing up to 1 m high. It has an erect and branching habit with pale green **leaves**. The lower leaves are two or three-pinnatifid, the upper leaves are flat with long, narrow teeth. Double, semi-double or single **flowers**, 4–7 cm across, range from white to golden yellow and have a pleasant smell of camomile. Flowering is in spring and summer. This is a strong and aggressive daisy that will quickly populate open, grassy or wasteland areas and is also grown in private gardens. In temperate climates and fertile soils, plants have been known to reach 2 m in height. Garland daisy is commonly grown as an ornamental in the Western world, with the name *coronarium* meaning 'used for or belonging to garlands'. The species *Chrysanthemum spatiosum* is cultivated as a vegetable in China and Japan where it is known as shunkigu daisy or chop suey greens.

Cosmos *Cosmos bipinnatus*

Family Compositae/Asteracae. Comos is an annual originating from Mexico and from a genus of 25 species. This is a tall-growing, bushy plant that will reach 90–150 cm high and around 45 cm wide. It has fine, feathery foliage. The pinnate, mid-green **leaves** are opposite and grow around 20 cm in length. The flowering stems are topped with white, pink or rosy-red **flowers**. The single or semi-double, daisy-like flowers are 8–10 cm across with wide, serrated petals circling a yellow centre. Flowering is from late spring to autumn. Cosmos, introduced to Europe at the end of the 18th century, is an old-time favourite of country gardens. In New Zealand it can be found in meadow gardens and home gardens where it freely self-seeds. In warmer areas it can flower all winter and can happily colonise itself in heavy clay soils and can compete aggressively with weeds and grasses.

Sweet William *Dianthus barbatus*

Family Caryophyllaceae. A native of Europe, this plant is biennial in cool climates, perennial in warm climates. It grows from dense, evergreen, basal tufts to 30–45 cm high, spreading around 30 cm. Each plant has rosettes of wide, green lanceolate **leaves**.

Strong stems are topped with dense, slightly rounded clusters of five-petalled **flowers**, 2 cm across. Flowers are pinkish-purple or red and are finely spotted with white. Some flowers have eyes or zones of contrasting colours and all have a sweet, clove-like fragrance. Plants can be found growing in private gardens, clearings and meadows, flowering in summer to autumn. Sweet William has been grown in gardens since at least the 16th century. This close relative of the carnation is a wildflower that was taken directly into gardens from the wild. Almost all dianthus have been cultivated for so long, and are now so diverse, that some bear little relation to the wild species. The word *Dianthus* comes from combining the Greek words 'dios', divine, and 'anthos', flower, an allusion to their heavenly fragrance and colour.

Gazania *Gazania splendens*

Family Asteraceae. *Gazania splendens* is a herbaceous perennial native to South Africa. The plant grows 20–30 cm high in a mounded clump that over time spreads in size to create a mat-like form. The spathulate **leaves** are 10 cm or longer, often with coarsely lobed margins. They have a glossy, dark green upper surface with a silky white, woolly underside. The solitary **flowers** are produced on long stalks known as peduncles. Each flower has an arrangement of disc flowers creating a centre eye with more colourful ray petals radiating around the eye. The flower can be up to 8 cm across and is usually orange or yellow, often with black or white spots at the base of the ray petals. The blooms close up at night or during cloudy weather. Flowering can occur throughout the year, but is most pronounced during the cooler months of spring and autumn. Plants can be found in warm, coastal districts, often colonising sand dunes where they are planted for stabilisation. *Gazania* can also be found in coastal home gardens, roadsides and sometimes even surviving in lawns. There are a large number of cultivars of this species.

Family Balsaminaceae. Impatiens is an annual, sometimes perennial, plant originating from the mountains in tropical Africa. It is a bushy plant growing 20–50 cm high and 30–40 cm wide. There are over 600 species in the genus. Succulent stems bear medium-green **leaves**, ovate to elliptic, toothed, often with a reddish tint, 2 to 6 cm long. White, red, violet, pink, orange or multi-coloured **flowers**, 2–4 cm wide, are flat with five equal-sized petals. Each flower has a narrow spur, 3–4 cm long, curving backwards. The **seedpods** will pop open when touched, liberally spreading their seeds around. This plant will flower almost year round in warm areas of the country where it seeds down prolifically. It can be found colonising shady areas in home gardens, parks and reserves and sometimes in waste areas. There are literally hundreds of forms that have hybridised from this plant in all colours, flower forms and sizes. Another common name is busy Lizzie.

Family Scrophulariaceae. Native to Morocco, this annual plant has an erect, branching habit growing 30–60 cm high and 20–30 cm wide. Mid-green, narrow, linear **leaves** are 3–4 cm long and grow on slender, upright stems. The **flowers** grow in terminal racemes from the leaf axils all the way up the stems, finishing in a cluster at the terminal of the stem. The snapdragon-like flowers

are in a multitude of colours from yellow, white, pink and red to purple and some multi-colours. Each flower is 1–2 cm wide with a yellow eye and a white or yellow blotch on the lower lip. A characteristic 1 cm-long spur is found at the back of the flower. Small oblong **seed** capsules hold thousands of minute black seeds, up to 15,000 per gram. The plant is a rapid bloomer, flowering in spring to early summer and can be found naturalising in home gardens and wildflower meadows. When flowering en masse *Linaria* presents a kaleidoscope of colour. The plant is also commonly known as spurred snapdragon, with the flowers being like miniature snapdragon flowers from the *Antirrhinum* species.

MIXED

Family Fabaceae. This perennial, native to western North America, grows to a height of 1–1.5 m with a spread of 45–60 cm. Large, long-stalked, palmate **leaves** are divided into 9–17 leaflets. Flowering spikes shoot high above the mid-green foliage. The **flowers** are arranged in whorls on racemes 15–60 cm long in colours of blue, orange, pink, purple, red, white and yellow. Some flower racemes are one solid colour and some are bi-coloured. Lupins are traditional cottage garden plants, blooming from early to mid-summer. The Russell lupin is named after George Russell of Yorkshire, England, who through vigorous selection bred amazing colour and form into some of the more common ancestors of the forms we have today. Russell lupins have aggressively colonised many central South Island riverbeds and roadsides, providing a beautiful and often spectacular sight. This is surely one of this country's most celebrated wildflowers, so much so that it is often mistakenly thought to be a New Zealand native. Lupins are a legume and are related to beans, peas, carob, peanuts, honey locusts, vetch and clover.

Marvel of Peru *Mirabilis jalapa*

Family Nyctaginaceae. There is some disagreement about the origin of this plant but it is generally thought to be from the tropical parts of America. *Mirabilis* is an annual, sometimes perennial, plant that reaches a height of 60–90 cm from a tuberous root. It is a bushy, fast-growing plant with erect, branching stems and mid-green, oval to lanceolate **leaves**. Trumpet-shaped, 2–3 cm-wide **flowers** are red, pink, purple, yellow and white, sometimes with different colours on the same plant. The sweet-scented flowers usually open mid to late afternoon and fade the following morning. Sometimes during cool or dull weather flowers will open earlier. Flowering takes place from mid-summer to autumn. Plants are more commonly found in warmer temperate areas, mostly in home gardens, parks and reserves where they

seed profusely. Medicinal extracts were traditionally prepared from the tubers. *Mirabilis* is Latin for 'miraculous' or 'wonderful'. *Jalapa* is a town in Mexico where it was first recorded as far back as 1753. Another common name is four o'clock plant, which refers to the afternoon opening of the flowers.

MIXED

Primula malacoides, mauve flowers.

Family Primulaceae. This is a clump-forming annual from China and comes from a genus of approximately 400 species. In nature they are all perennial, but as they cannot tolerate extremes of temperature, particularly summer heat, many of the species are grown as annuals. Plants will grow 25–30 cm high and wide. Crinkled, pale green **leaves** form a neat basal rosette. Leaves are ovate with rounded teeth and grow 3–10 cm long. Slender flowering stems carry spikes of densely packed, tiny, single **flowers** above the foliage. The pink, mauve or white flowers, 5–15 mm across, grow in tiers and whorl around the stems. Each whorl has up to 20 flowers.

Primula malacoides, white flowers.

Flowering is in late winter and early spring. Plants will easily naturalise in semi-shaded garden areas and can be found through most areas of the country. There are many hybrids grown that have larger flowers in a wider colour range but these do not have the ability to seed down.

Cinereria *Senecio cruentus*

Family Asteraceae. Cinereria was originally native to the Canary Islands. It is a perennial plant, usually grown as an annual, reaching around 60 cm high and 30 cm wide. Mid to dark green and slightly bristly **leaves** are ovate to palmate, marginally toothed and tinged purple beneath. Large basal leaves are around 15 cm across and the upper leaves around 10 cm. Starry-style **flowers** are in large, rounded, dense trusses. The flower rays may be white, pink, rose, purple, blue or bi-coloured and surround a large, central disc. Each flower is around 5 cm across and flowering is in late winter and spring. Plants are commonly found naturalising in shady, frost-free areas, mostly in home gardens, parks and sometime in waste ground. Cinererias have been extensively hybridised and modified so it is doubtful if the plants here today are very true to the original. In 1772, Francis Masson, an English explorer from the Royal Botanical Gardens, went to the Canary Islands and gathered the original wild plants for greenhouse-produced cinereria. The plant name is also synonymous with *Pericallis* x *hybrida*.

Glossary

Alternate leaves that arise singly on alternate sides of the stem.

Annual a plant that completes its life cycle in one year or less.

Axil the angle between a leaf and a stem.

Basal term applied to leaves arising at the base of the plant stem.

Biennial a plant that completes its life cycle within two years.

Bract a scale or leaf-like modified leaf associated with a flower.

Bulb an underground storage organ consisting of fleshy leaf bases.

Calyx (plural calyces) outer protective part of a flower made up of sepals fused together.

Capsule a dry fruit that splits when ripe to shed its seeds.

Corolla inner protective part of a flower consisting of wholly or partly fused petals.

Cyme a rounded, domed or flattened cluster of flowers.

Deciduous referring to a plant that loses its leaves at the end of a growing season.

Disc domed or flattened centre of a daisy flower.

Dissected in the form of narrow lobes or segments.

Elliptic generally applied to leaves, meaning oval with narrowed ends.

Entire used to describe leaves or petals with smooth margins.

Evergreen referring to a plant that bears foliage throughout the year.

Falls drooping outer petals.

Floret a small individual flower that forms part of a larger flower.

Flower an organ composed of specialised parts for sexual reproduction.

Flower head a group of flowers clustered into a head.

Fruit the structure that contains ripe seeds of a plant.

Genus a group containing a number of allied species closely related by one or more distinctive features.

Gland a small globular structure containing liquid.

Glaucous usually a blue-grey, pale bloom, referring to leaves and stems.

Herbaceous usually applied to perennial plants that die down in the autumn and reappear in the spring.

Inflorescence the arrangement of one or more flowers on a plant.

Lanceolate applied to a narrow leaf, widest at the base and tapering to a point.

Lateral a stem or shoot that branches off from a bud in the leaf axil of a larger stem.

Leaf a main organ of a plant made up of a flat blade with or without a stalk.

Leaflet a single part of a leaf that is divided into separate leaf-like parts.

Linear a narrow leaf, bract or petal with parallel sides.

Lobe a protruding part of a leaf, petal, bract or sepal.

Nodes a stem joint from where leaves, buds and side shoots arise.

Nutlet a tiny nut.

Oblanceolate applied to a narrow leaf that is widest towards the tip. The reverse of lanceolate.

Obovate applied to an egg-shaped leaf with the widest part at the tip.

Opposite the arrangement of leaves that arise on opposite sides of the same point on a stem.

Ovate applied to an egg-shaped leaf with the widest part at the base. The reverse of obovate.

Palmate having five lobes or segments.

Panicle large, branched flower cluster with numerous, individually stalked flowers.

Pendant hanging or suspended.

Perennial a plant that completes its life cycle over a period of more than two years.

Petal the part of a flower immediately inside the sepals. It is leaf-like in shape and brightly coloured.

Pinnate a leaf that is divided into several pairs of oppositely arranged leaflets.

Prostrate lying along the ground.

Raceme a cylindrical head of stalked flowers.

Ray floret the strap or tongue-shaped outer floret of a daisy flower.

Recurved refers to leaves, branches or petals that arch or curve backwards.

Rhizome an underground, creeping horizontal stem.

Rosette a ring of leaves at the stem base.

Sap the life fluid of plants, mainly water with dissolved minerals and sugars.

Seed a reproductive unit developing from a fertilised flower.

Sepal the outermost parts of a flower that protect the flower when in bud.

Sessile without a stalk.

Spadix a slender, spike-like flower head usually surrounded by a spathe.

Spathe a green or coloured bract-like sheath enclosing a flower spike.

Spathulate a spoon-shaped leaf that is wide at the tip and tapers towards the base.

Species a group of individual plants that can breed together and have the same constant and distinctive characteristics although small differences can occur.

Spikelet parts of a branched flower head containing stalkless flowers.

Stamen the male reproductive organ of a flower.

Stipule a small leafy or scale-like structure at the base of the leaf stalk.

Stolon a prostrate, creeping stem rooting at nodes and giving rise to further stems or plantlets.

Taproot an unbranched root growing vertically downwards.

Tendril a modified stem or leaf that twines around supports to enable the plant to climb.

Terminal occurring at the end of a stem.

Tomentum a dense covering of short, firm, matted hairs.

Trifoliate having three leaves or leaflets.

Tuber a short, swollen part of an underground stem used for food storage.

Umbel a flower head in which all the flower stalks radiate outwards from a single point.

Whorl leaves or flowers arranged in a ring around a stem.

Further reading

Bishop, Owen and Audrey; photographs by Nic Bishop, *New Zealand Wild Flowers Handbook*, Hodder Moa Beckett Publishers, 2002.

California Flora plant names website: Latin name meanings and derivations: www.calflora.net/botanicalnames

Cave, Yvonne and Paddison, Valda, *The Gardener's Encyclopedia of Native Plants*, Godwit, 1999.

Johnson, Peter, *Pick of the Bunch: New Zealand Wildflowers*, Longacre Press, 1997.

Salmon, John, *Native New Zealand Flowering Plants*, Reed Publishing, 1991.

Wildflower World website: www.wildflowerworld.com

Index

Aaron's rod 95
Acaena species 96
Achillea millefolium 97
Aciphylla aurea 61
African daisy 77, 119, 124
African lily 12
agapanthus 12
Agapanthus africanus 12
Agrostemma coeli-rosa 58
Alchemilla mollis 62
Allium triquetrum 98
alpine strawberry 112
Alstroemeria aurantiaca 63
   aurea 63
Ammi majus 99, 109
Anagallis arvensis 64
Anaphalis keriense 100
   rupestris 100
Anemone japonica 101
Arctotheca calendula 65
arctotis 124
Arctotis stoechadifolia 124
Arthropodium candidum 102
   cirratum 102
Arum italicum 103
arum lily 123

baby blue eyes 28
baby's breath 113
bachelor's button 13, 74
Bellis perennis 104
biddybid 96
bidibidi 96
Billy buttons 49
bishop's flower 99
bitter herb 36
black-eyed Susan 93
blanket flower 82
blue flax 23
blueberry 110
brass buttons 74
breath of heaven 58
Briza maxima 105
   media 105
   minor 105
Bulbinella hookeri 66
busy Lizzie 130
butter and eggs 22
buttercup 90
buttonweed 74

calendula 67
Calendula officinalis 67
Californian poppy 79
Canna indica 125
canna lily 125
cape marigold 77
cape weed 65
Carpobrotus edulis 68
catchfly 57
Celmisia semicordata 106
   specatablis 106

Centaurea cyanus 13
Centaurium erythraea 36
centaury 36
Centranthus ruber 37
Chatham Island forget-me-not
   26
cheese flower 49
chicory 14
Chinese forget-me-not 16
Chinese hound's tongue 16
chop suey greens 126
Chrysanthemum coronarium 126
   leucanthemum 107, 108
   maximum 108
   segetum 69
   spatiosum 126
Cichorium intybus 14
cineraria 135
Clarkia amoena 38
common helichrysum 114
common mallow 49
common thyme 60
Coreopsis lanceolata 70
   tinctoria 71
corn marigold 69
corn poppy 52
cornflower 13
Corydalis lutea 72
cosmos 73, 127
Cosmos bipinnatus 73, 127
   sulphureus 73
cotton daisy 106
Cotula coronopifolia 74
Cotyledon orbiculata 75
cranesbill 41
creeping buttercup 90
creeping brookweed 122
creeping pratia 121
Crocosmia x *crocosmiiflora* 76
cudweed 100
cushion spurge 80
Cymbalaria muralis 15
Cynoglossum amabile 16

dame's rocket 19
dame's violet 19
Daucus carota 99, 109
Dianella intermedia 110
   nigra 110
Dianthus barbatus 128
Digitalis purpurea 17
dimorphotheca 77, 119
Dimorphotheca aurantiaca 77
   sinuata 77
Disphyma australe 39
dog rose 55
Duchesnea indica 78
Dyer's rocket 92

Echium plantagineum 18
   vulgare 18
eglantine 55

English bluebell 20
English marigold 67
Erigeron karvinskianus 111
Eschscholzia californica 79
Euphorbia amygdaloides 80
   glauca 40
   polychroma 80
   var. *robbiae* 80
evening primrose 89
everlasting daisy 114
everlasting pea 45

fairy primrose 134
farewell to spring 38
fennel 81
feverwort 36
five spot 28
Flanders poppy 51
fleur de Lys 86
flower de Luce 86
Foeniculum vulgare 81
forget-me-not 27
four o'clock plant 133
foxglove 17
Fragaria vesca 112

Gaillardia aristata 82
   pulchella 82
garden thyme 60
garland daisy 126
Gazania splendens 129
gazania 129
Geranium maderense 41
   robertianum 41, 42
giant buttercup 90
gloriosa daisy 93
godetia 38
golden Spaniard 61
golden speargrass 61
gravel groundsel 32
greater periwinkle 34
greater quaking grass 105
Gypsophila elegans 113
   paniculata 113

harakeke 53
heartsease 35
hedge woundwort 59
Helichrysum belliodides 114
   intermedium 114
herb Robert 42
Hesperis matrionalis 19
Hibiscus diversifolius 83
   trionum 83
Himalayan balsam 43
honesty 24
horokaka 39
Hottentot fig 68
Hyacinthoides hispanica 20
   non-scripta 20
Hypericum perforatum 84

ice plant 39, 68
impatiens 130

Impatiens glandulifera 43
   walleriana 130
Indian blanket 82
Indian shot 125
Indian strawberry 78
Iris foetidissima 85
   japonica 21
   pseudacorus 86
Italian arum 103
ivy-leaved toadflax 15

Japanese anemone 101
Japanese iris 21
Johnny jump ups 35
Jovellana sinclairii 115

Kniphofia uvaria 44

lacy phacelia 31
lady's mantle 62
large-flowered mallow 49
Lathyrus latifolius 45
   odoratus 45
lawn daisy 104
lesser periwinkle 34
Leucanthemum vulgare 107
libertia 116
Libertia grandiflora 116
   ixioides 116
   peregrinans 116
Linaria maroccana 131
   purpurea 22
   vulgaris 22
Linum grandiflorum rubrum 46
   perenne lewisii 23
   usitatissimum 23
Lobularia maritima 117
long-headed poppy 50
lords and ladies 103
love in a mist 29
Lunaria annua 24
lupin 87, 132
Lupinus arboreus 87
   polyphyllus 132
Lychnis coronaria 47
   coronaria alba 47
Lythrum salicaria 48

maakoako 122
Malcomia maritima 25
mallow 49
Malva sylvestris 49
Maori calceolaria 115
Maori onion 66
marigold 67
marvel of Peru 133
Mazus radicans 118
   pumilio 118
Mesembryanthemum australe 39
   edule 68
Mexican daisy 111
mignonette 92
Mimulus guttatus 88
   moschatus 88

repens 88
Mirabilis jalapa 133
money plant 24
monkey musk 88
montbretia 76
Montbretia crocosmia 76
moth mullein 95
mountain daisy 106
mountain flax 53
mountain pinatoro 120
mountain pratia 121
mullein 95
Myosotidium hortensia 26
Myosotis sylvatica 27

native ice plant 39
Nemophila maculata 28
  menziesii 28
New Zealand daphne 120
New Zealand flax 53
New Zealand iris 116
Nigella damascena 29
none-so-pretty 57

Oenothera biennis 89
  glazioviana 89
  lamarckiana 89
  stricta 89
onion weed 98
Osteospermum fruticosum 119
oxeye daisy 107, 108

panakenake 121
pancake plant 49
pansy 35
Papaver dubium 50
  rhoeas 50, 51, 52
Parochetus communis 30
Paterson's curse 18
perennial hibiscus 83
perennial pea 45
Pericallis x *hybrida* 135
periwinkle 34
Peruvian lily 63
Phacelia tanacetifolia 31
Phormium cookianum 53
  tenax 53
pig face 68
pig's ear 75
Pimelia oreophila 120
  prostrata 120
pink head knotweed 54
piripiri 96
plains coreopsis 71
policeman's helmet 43
Polygonum capitatum 54
poor man's weather glass 64
poppy 50, 51
pot marigold 67
Pratia angulata 121
  macrodon 121
  physaloides 121
Primula malacoides 134
puatea 100

purple groundsel 32
purple linaria 22
purple loosestrife 48
purple tansy 31
purple top 33

quaking grass 105
Queen Anne's lace 99, 109

Ranunculus acris 90
  repens 90
Raoulia species 91
red hot poker 44
red poppy 51
red valerian 37
reinga lily 102
rengarenga 102
Reseda alba 92
  lutea 92
  luteola 92
rock lily 102
Rosa canina 55
  rubiginosa 55
rose campion 47
rose of heaven 58
rose silene 58
Rudbeckia hirta 93
Russell lupin 132

Salvia coccinea 56
Samolus repens 122
sand spurge 40
scabweeds 91
scarlet flax 46
scarlet pimpernel 64
scarlet sage 56
Scilla non-scripta 20
Sedum acre 94
Senecio cruentus 135
  elegans 32
  skirrhodon 32
shamrock pea 30
shasta daisy 108
Shirley poppy 52
shivery grass 105
shore spurge 40
shunkigu daisy 126
Silene armeria 57
  coeli-rosa 58
smartweed 54
soldier poppy 51
Spanish bluebell 20
spurred snapdragon 131
Stachys sylvatica 59
star lily 102
star of the Veldt 77
stinking iris 85
St John's wort 84
stonecrop 94
swamp musk 118
sweet alyssum 117
sweet briar 55
sweet rocket 19
sweet William 128

taramea 61
thyme 60
Thymus vulgaris 60
tickseed 70
toadflax 131
trailing African daisy 119
tree lupin 87
turutu 110

valerian 37
vegetable sheep 91
Verbascum thapsus 95
   virgatum 95
Verbena bonariensis 33
Vinca major 34
   minor 34
Viola tricolor 35
viper's bugloss 18
Virginia stock 25
viscaria 58
Viscaria oculata 58

weld 92
wharariki 53
wild carrot 99, 109
wild garlic 98
wild pansy 35
wild strawberry 112
wild thyme 60
windflower 101
wood spurge 80

yarrow 97
yellow buttons 74
yellow corydalis 72
yellow cosmos 73
yellow flag iris 86

Zantedeschia aethiopica 123